This book does an excellent job of putting into words what most of us working in law enforcement did for many years and found effective. The Deconfliction Principles are something I utilized in my almost 22 years of law enforcement experience without actually thinking about them.

Michael W. Knox
Deputy Sheriff (Retired)
Federal Explosives Specialist (Current)

Marc's years of successful law enforcement experience is quite evident throughout each well-thought out chapter. The real-life stories and experiences capture exactly what this book is about and prove Deconfliction is a viable course of action. In a newsworthy discipline where few quality resources are available, this is a must-read.

Marc Dolphin, Special Agent (Retired)

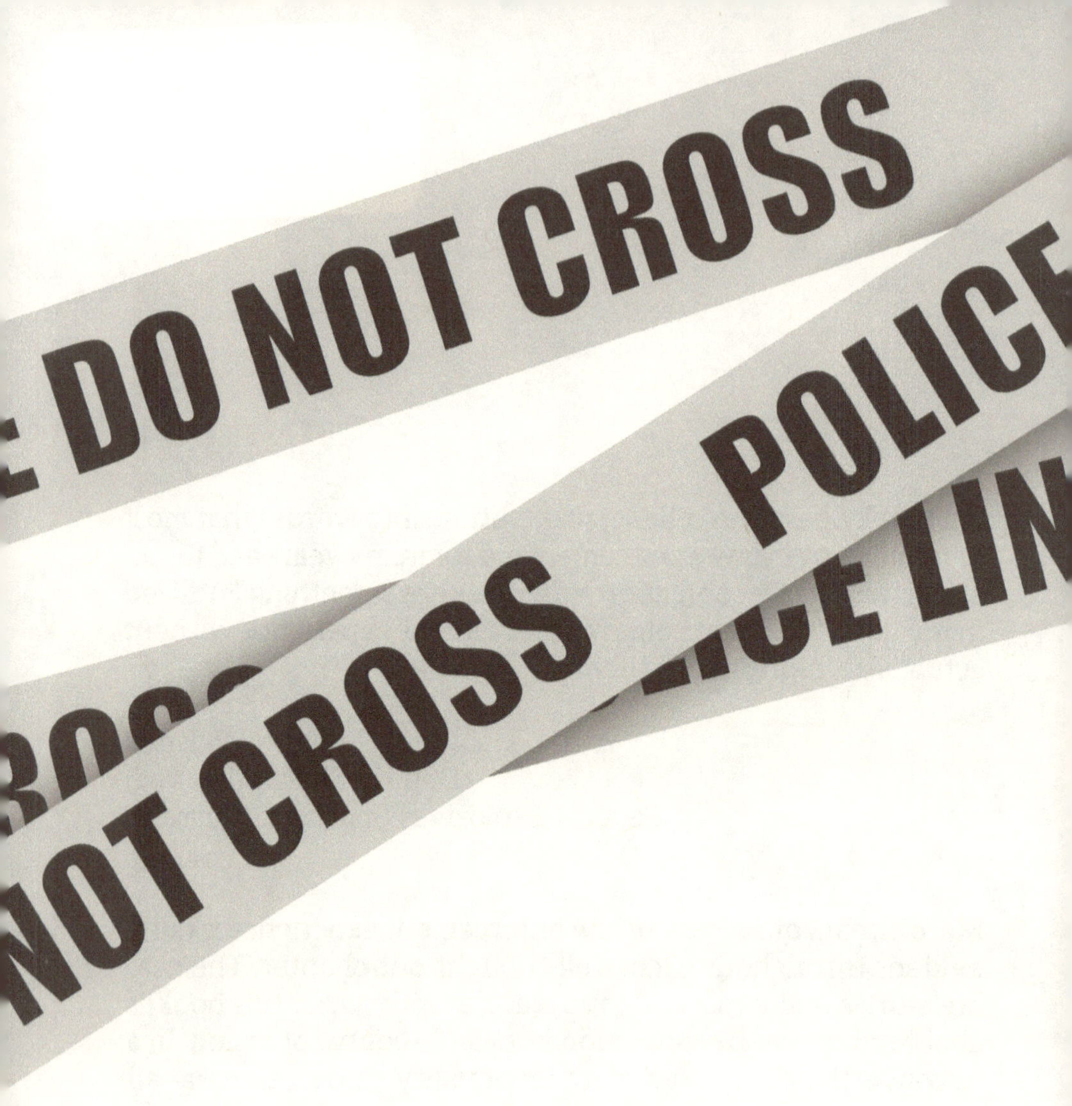
DO NOT CROSS
NOT CROSS
POLICE

DECONFLICTION
DON'T BE A STATISTIC

MARC ZELINSKY

Deconfliction: Don't Be a Statistic
Copyright © 2025 Marc Zelinsky. All rights reserved.

Published By: 4 Horsemen Publications, Inc.

4 Horsemen Publications, Inc.
PO Box 417
Sylva, NC 28779
4horsemenpublications.com
info@4horsemenpublications.com

Edited by Jen Paquette

All rights to the work within are reserved to the author and publisher. No part of this publication may be reproduced, stored in a retrieval system, or transmitted in any form or by any means, electronic, mechanical, photocopying, recording, scanning, or otherwise, except as permitted under Section 107 or 108 of the 1976 International Copyright Act, without prior written permission except in brief quotations embodied in critical articles and reviews. Please contact either the Publisher or Author to gain permission.

All characters, organizations, and events portrayed in this novel are either products of the author's imagination or are used fictitiously.

No generative artificial intelligence was used in the creation of this book or its cover.

All brands, quotes, and cited work respectfully belongs to the original rights holders and bear no affiliation to the authors or publisher.

The views presented are those of the author and do not necessarily represent the views of DoD or the Army.

Library of Congress Control Number: 2025945787

Paperback ISBN-13: 979-8-8232-1000-3
Hardcover ISBN-13: 979-8-8232-1001-0
Ebook ISBN-13: 979-8-8232-1002-7

DEDICATION

For all those who died in the line of duty and those citizens who were wrongfully killed during a police encounter. Also, for my dearly departed mother Patricia. She was an inspiration.

FOREWORD

This book does an excellent job of putting into words what most of us working in law enforcement did for many years and found effective. The Deconfliction Principles are something I utilized in my almost 22 years of law enforcement experience without actually thinking about them. I found them useful in every position I was assigned before retirement: patrol, narcotics, intelligence, training, S.W.A.T. commander, bomb squad commander, and a few more spots I have forgotten. I have known Marc Zelinsky for over 10 years, and I can say, without hesitation, he was always a consummate professional and thoughtful about performing his duties. If anyone was going to identify and explain the principles of deconfliction it would be Marc based upon his experience and educational background. Mr. Zelinsky, whom I've had the pleasure supervising as patrol deputy and commanding when he was a member of the S.W.A.T sniper element, has laid out the Deconfliction Principles in a very clear, concise and easy to comprehend manner that cops and citizens alike should find appetizing.

I understand that most citizens today expect more from public servants and want a complete explanation for everything an officer is asking or telling them to do. Some citizens claim they can do or say anything they want, and it's the job of the law enforcement officer to remain professional and courteous. However, citizens do have an obligation to cooperate with lawful orders and should display some manners. Although the same rules don't really apply to them, imploring them to use the same approach as well-trained police officers is to their benefit. From my perspective, Mr. Zelinsky's Deconfliction Principles lay out everything law enforcement officers and citizens need to know in an easy-to-follow outline. I think we are well past the time to adopt the Deconfliction Principles as times have changed.

Deconfliction touches on the sensitive subject of systemic racism in the criminal justice system, highlighting the wavetops without delving into an entire book on the subject. Mr. Zelinsky sorts through some of the confusing definitions and terms on the matter and leaves the door open for real honest discussion. In my experience, most cops don't have racial prejudices but cultural ones. It becomes an "us vs. them" attitude, sometimes out of a survival instinct and sometimes as a matter of accepted practice. At that point, race becomes irrelevant. Even minority officers might feel that way toward people of their own race because they "aren't part of the team."

In short, I would recommend all those who carry a badge and a gun for a living delve headlong into this book and maximize their effectiveness as a cop by adopting Mr. Zelinsky's Deconfliction Principles as part of their problem-solving repertoire. I would also suggest that citizens would benefit immensely by using these principles as well. After all, cops aren't the only people who have to deal with others every day. Mr. Zelinsky's Deconfliction Principles will not only help you out if you encounter a law enforcement officer, but these concepts are useful in life in general. If everyone utilized these ideas daily, conflict would take a backseat to working together to solve problems.

Michael W. Knox
Deputy Sheriff (Retired)
Federal Explosives Specialist (Current)

CONTENTS

PROLOGUE .... **XI**

CHAPTER 1: STARTING POINT **1**
    Author background
    Problems with de-escalation
    The demonization of police before, during, and after 2020
    Frustrations with the commentary on law enforcement

CHAPTER 2: LAW ENFORCEMENT PERSPECTIVE **13**
    Mindset of police in general regarding police/citizen interaction
    Unrealistic expectations of police
    Product of their environment training evolution in general

CHAPTER 3: REALITIES OF TRAINING **25**
    Force continuum explanation
    De-escalation: What police are really taught
    Deconfliction outline

CHAPTER 4: DECONFLICTION PRINCIPLES **39**
    Situational awareness
    Use your words
    Active listening
    Empathy
    Find common ground
    Acknowledge the problem
    Confront negative feelings

Encourage compromise
Give choices
Be polite

CHAPTER 5: DECONFLICTION PRINCIPLES IN ACTION 59
Personal examples using de-confliction

CHAPTER 6: SYSTEMIC RACISM IN LAW ENFORCEMENT 75
Fact-Fiction-Reality

CHAPTER 7: MENTAL HEALTH CRISIS 89
Interactions during a mental health crisis

CHAPTER 8: TRAINING EVOLUTION 97
How training has evolved naturally (as opposed to by force)

CHAPTER 9: CITIZEN DUTY (DON'T BECOME A STATISTIC) 107
Citizens need to deconflict a situation as well
The challenge culture

CHAPTER 10: REIMAGINE POLICING 115
Police reimagined
National police standards
The "Thin Blue Liability"

REFERENCES 127

AUTHOR BIO 139

PROLOGUE

> "Out of suffering have emerged the strongest souls; the most massive characters are seared with scars."
>
> –Khalil Gibran

"266, dispatch, in service, district seven."

"Dispatch, copy."

It was just before 0600 hours on another beautiful Sunday morning in Charleston, South Carolina, and I was on my way to my district in West Ashley. It was the last day of a three-day stretch of 12-hour shifts. West Ashley, a suburb of Charleston, had greatly expanded since I started with the Charleston City Police back in 2002. Now, I was a deputy sheriff with the Charleston County Sheriff's Office, a field training instructor, and waiting for my transfer to the detective division.

I stopped at the Sheriff's Office Law Enforcement Center, also known as the (LEC), to check my mailbox and check in with Jason, my partner. We had been working in the same district for a while now, and he became my "work wife," or so they told me. Jason and I had about 30 years of experience between us. Sundays in West Ashley, a city with a population of approximately 80,000 in 2018, were never predictable. We patrolled separately and had about 45 square miles to cover. Charleston

DECONFLICTION: DON'T BE A STATISTIC

City Police had jurisdiction over much of the area, but they had about eight officers per shift.

Jason and I usually attempted to stop for brunch on Sundays. Unfortunately, this was not one of those days.

"Dispatch, 266 and 94."

"94."

"266."

"Respond to the area of North Edgewater drive and Island drive. We have a report of a white male, mid-thirties, running around the neighborhood attempting to break into houses."

"94, copy code 1."

"266, copy code 1."

"Dispatch, 94, 266, we are getting additional calls. The subject tried to force his way into a passing truck and was dragged along the road. Additionally, a female caller stated she knew the subject; he started acting crazy this morning after drinking all weekend. He's schizophrenic, and she thinks he stopped taking his medication."

"Copy."

"266, 94, I'm a few minutes out, so you may want to hang back."

"94, dispatch I'm in the area."

Fuck. So much for hanging back, Jason. I guess we're not going for breakfast today.

Jason was searching for the subject as I hit the lights and siren to move past some traffic. A few minutes later, I arrived in the area.

"266, 94, if you're checking by the residence, I will check on Island Drive."

"94, Copy."

"266, dispatch. I have the subject here on Island Drive."

"Dispatch, copy."

"94, I copy."

Within a minute after turning onto Island Drive, I spotted the subject kneeling down in a driveway and punching the ground. I stopped about a house away from where the subject was assaulting the pavement and stepped out of my clearly marked police cruiser. The bright yellow badge on my

PROLOGUE

gray uniform revealed who I was or so I thought. The subject stood and walked toward the middle of the street. He was not wearing shoes.

"Hey man," I called out.

"Hey, hey, hey, hello," he replied in a very high-pitched voice, surprise showing on his face.

This dude is clearly out of his mind. I hope this goes well.

"Hey man. Do you know who I am?"

"No, no, no. Who are you?" he said rapidly, his tone still elevated.

"I'm a Charleston County Sheriff's Deputy. Can you come over here and talk to me?" I pointed to the front of my cruiser.

"Yeah, okay, okay, okay."

There has been a shift in law enforcement training from using force to de-escalation. Over the years, I have had countless hours of both types of training. I also have my own experiences as a law enforcement officer. At times, training and experience can be at odds. De-escalation? Something about the word de-escalation has always bothered me, but I never really gave it much thought. Policing is regulated by policies, "if A then B." There is a policy for just about everything. I had dealt with diagnosed and undiagnosed mentally ill people plenty of times. I was up on all the latest "training."

I was standing by the driver's door of my police cruiser, and the subject started toward the front of my cruiser in a cartoonish speed-walking kind of fashion with his arms flailing like an inflatable dancing character outside of a business. I thought I had a good buffer from the mentally unstable guy. Suddenly, seemingly channeling the Road Runner, he slipped around the front of my cruiser and barreled down on me like I was Wile E. Coyote. Briefly, I thought he would stop and salute like he was reporting for duty. The thought was fleeting.

Damn it!

In an instant, the scene went from cordial to downright hostile. Unpredictability is a common scenario in policing; however, there are those who believe unambiguous situations are the norm in police work. They obviously haven't dealt with an unhinged, off his medication, intoxicated schizophrenic who, as we found out later, had been dropping acid.

Defending myself with a few carefully chosen fanciful de-escalation words was not an option. Also, I had no time to contemplate the use of one of three less than lethal devices attached to my utility belt. I settled on an *oh shit* arms-up blocking technique. This definitely was not covered in defensive tactics training.

Fuck!

He slammed into me, and we tumbled to the ground. I rolled back over to a sitting position. The next thing I knew he had crawled across my body and attempted to extricate my Glock 22 from its holster.

Every call for service a police officer responds to is a gun call. How, you ask? The officer brings the gun.

Fortunately, there is extensive training for just this type of situation.

A slow-motion feeling washed over me as I sat on the ground regaining my bearings. I reflexively latched onto the top and side of my holster, which is taught and practiced every year in police defensive tactics training, as he tugged at my gun, trying to pull it free.

What the hell does he think he is doing? He can't get my gun out. I'm glad I started keeping my knife near my holster. I may need it. Where the hell is Jason?

Then, without warning, he released his grip from my gun and growled, "Nah, I'm not going to do that." He scrambled to his feet and stood hovering over me.

I stayed seated on the ground. I wanted to avoid a repeat of earlier events which found me sprawled out on the pavement. At this point, there was no talking, no de-escalating the situation. I was in it.

He hovered only a few feet away from me, and perhaps he was contemplating a second attack. I partially drew my handgun from its holster, fearing another strike.

My peripheral vision was quickly filled with the grill of a police cruiser fast approaching. The cavalry had arrived!

PROLOGUE

Damn it, Jason! Don't run me over!

Consciously, I re-holstered my handgun and drew my Taser. I leaned up toward the subject and deployed the 50,000 volts of muscle-contracting electricity. The probes fired and found their mark, just about midsection.

The Taser had little effect; however, Jason, a defensive tactics instructor, was able to wrestle him to the ground. In a case of bad luck, Jason became entangled in the Taser wires, and since I did not release the trigger from sheer adrenaline, Jason was the second person I Tased that day.

Jason yelled "STOP" a few times. For a second, I thought he was using his de-escalation training on the subject. Turns out, he was yelling at me to stop, and I let go of the trigger for the Taser.

Sorry, Jason.

"Dispatch, 266 or 94."

(Radio silence)

(Emergency tone)

Jason and I were a little busy trying to secure handcuffs on the subject, who was still fighting, and he showed amazing strength. The subject continued to struggle despite Jason having his shoulder and arm held firmly in place with an advanced defensive tactics maneuver. I eventually secured his hands in handcuffs, which only slowed him down. Fire and EMS, who watched the events unfold like an episode of *COPS*, were on scene because the original call indicated injuries, which required they be dispatched as well. Policy dictated EMS wait until the situation was secure.

The subject would rise up and attempt to stand up even though he was in handcuffs and all 200 pounds of Jason and gear were holding him down. A few firefighters jumped in to assist. *Policy violation appreciated.*

The paramedics were on the radio with the doctor at the local hospital asking for permission to administer a dose of Ketamine to the subject, a powerful sedative.

Approved!

A large amount of Ketamine was injected, so I was told later. The drug had minimal effect on the subject. The incident went from wrestling an alligator to fighting with a feral cat.

The paramedics took over and loaded him onto a gurney and strapped him down. We were informed later by other deputies who went to the hospital with the subject he cursed everyone all the way to and at the hospital.

We did not file assault charges or any charges against the guy for that matter. Frankly, I was not anxious to see him in court.

The profession of law enforcement has the *joie de vivre* many people are looking for in a career. In policing, you never know. A quiet Sunday can turn into a fight for your life.

Although, I never really felt I was in grave danger. Maybe it was my training or life experiences which kept me calm and seemingly in control of the situation. I will discuss this ability or lack of ability to remain calm in a crisis situation more in depth later.

Police encounter many different individuals every day all day, the ending of which could definitely be a surprise. On that particular day, I was armed with the information. The subject was suffering from schizophrenia, and the outcome was still uncertain.

My first thought when I arrived was that I should be able to talk this guy down off the ledge. How very wrong I was.

De-escalation and the techniques taught along with it, which is the current prevailing training received by law enforcement, has a fundamental flaw within the initial situational premise.

In contrast, Deconfliction and the Deconfliction Principles are a complete mindset.

My penultimate goal with this book is to pull back the curtain on police-citizen interactions. The ultimate objective in developing Deconfliction and the Deconfliction Principles is a positive contribution to the profession of law enforcement.

CHAPTER 1

STARTING POINT

"Afternoon, license, registration, and insurance, please. Do you know why I pulled you over?"

My standard opening. If you heard it, I had just initiated a traffic stop, and you were the offender. The next several minutes were crucial. I was making an assessment regarding any potential threats to my safety. If this process sounds easy, simple, like common sense, then you have never experienced the real complexities of a "routine" traffic stop, or someone has not explained the nuances.

It is frustrating listening to comments by pundits regarding what a police officer should have done during a citizen encounter. Additionally, it's heartbreaking to hear when the media elicits a heartfelt assertion such as, "I'm afraid for my child when they are stopped by police." The sadness comes from knowing what is actually going through the mind of the officer during a traffic stop, and the anxiety family members experience each time their loved one dons the uniform and walks out the door. The simple solution is for mutual recognition by all parties to a traffic stop that each has some level of angst during this encounter. Empathy, respect, and a little politeness can go a long way.

"Afternoon. I'm Deputy Zelinsky with the Charleston County Sheriff's Office. May I see your license, registration, and insurance? Do you know why I pulled you over?"

"This is some fucking bullshit. No, I don't know why you fucking pulled me over."

Nice language with the kids in the car.

"Well, ma'am, you ran the red light, right in front of me actually. I know this because my light turned green before you entered the intersection. You didn't see me? I was the first car at the light?"

"No, I didn't fucking see you."

"Okay, give me a few minutes."

This book is predicated on giving context to situations and practices of the law enforcement profession. Optimistically, genuine rhetorical and actual questions will arise. My goal is to give some possible explanations of why police-citizen interactions go horribly wrong, and ultimately, I will try and provide a practical approach to those encounters which will hopefully reduce those tragic outcomes.

If I were reading this book, the writer's background would be my first inquiry to determine if they had any practical knowledge of which they speak. What follows, a résumé of sorts, is for perspective. I've done my 10,000 hours (Gladwell, 2008).

My educational background starts with a bachelor's degree in criminology, followed by a juris doctorate 11 years later, and then a master's in criminal justice with a homeland security focus 11 years after the JD curiously enough. My practical experience started in the military as an officer, but not in law enforcement. Eventually, I migrated to Charleston, South Carolina in 2002, and I began my law enforcement career with the Charleston City Police. I worked in a high crime and drug

CHAPTER 1

area where various narcotics were sold. Cries of "five-o" and "one time" could be heard throughout the neighborhood.[1]

I departed Charleston briefly to work in Florida, which gave me a glimpse of how other police departments operated. It's actually interesting how policing is conducted in a comparable manner throughout the country due in part to the certifications by various organizations such as the Commission on Accreditation for Law Enforcement Agencies (CLEA).

I left the Charleston City Police in 2009 to do my part in the ongoing war against terrorism. I deployed to Afghanistan as a police advisor working with the Afghan National Police. For the next 18 months, I served alongside some cheeky British soldiers in Helmand Province, and then I was attached to an outstanding Illinois National Guard Military Police unit and the 82nd Airborne in Kandahar Province. While in Afghanistan, I was also very fortunate to be teamed up with Joel E., my longtime friend and police colleague.

After some baptisms of fire, my comfort level in Afghanistan ended, so I returned to Charleston and started working for the Charleston County Sheriff's Office in 2011. Almost eight months later, I took a contract position in Haiti. The job was advertised as a police advisor; however, it turned into an assignment with the United Nations watching over Haitians living in displacement camps around Port-au-Prince after the massive 2010 earthquake. You can't spell unorganized without UN—my personal take on how the United Nations internally administers peacekeeping operations.

I stayed in Haiti for one year after which I rejoined the Charleston County Sheriff's Office, as a patrol deputy. A few years later, I took on the responsibilities of a field training instructor teaching new deputies for almost two years. Additionally, I was

---

[1] Yelling "5-0" and "one time" were ways lookouts would warn the drug dealers the POPO (Police) were in the area. When Nextel phones were introduced, the sound of "beep beep" could be heard through the neighborhoods where narcotics were sold on the corner. Selling on the street corner has largely gone by the wayside, and dealers meet people at various locations through text messages.

selected for the SWAT team and then the sniper element. My last position in law enforcement was as a detective investigating child sexual and physical abuse along with adult sexual assault. I departed law enforcement in 2019.

Years of declining courteous regard from the public and the media began to weigh heavily on my desire for a new chapter. Additional to the deterioration of consideration from the public was the disrespect from within. Law enforcement had transformed predominantly into a liability adverse endeavor, which at times manifested as a less than professional contempt toward the rank-in-file demonstrated by high-level commanders. In the end, an opportunity arrived that took me outside of policing. Although I left law enforcement, a constant dissatisfaction remained with the commentary related to how policing is accomplished in general and assessments about specific events. Police work, by its nature, is nuanced.

I staged a comeback into law enforcement, although very brief, in 2023 when I was fortunate enough to be sent to the Federal Law Enforcement Training Centers (FLETC) in lovely Brunswick, Georgia. I attended and graduated from the Criminal Investigator Training Program (CITP) twelve-week course. This training program is attended by agents from over 100 federal agencies. The program is challenging, rigorous, and comprehensive. Many of the instructors were top notch, and the curriculum was extensive; however, just as there were shortcomings at the state academy level, federal training had similar deficiencies. This is somewhat of a self-serving statement considering the premise of this book, but I only want to improve police-citizen interactions.

Continuing, I worked for years without really conducting a deep analysis into the particulars of performing my job. I learned a few things over the years the hard way, such as don't assume that just because I have flashing blue lights and a loud-ass siren, people will see and hear me coming. And even if they do, they probably won't get out of my way.

Early on, I also learned I really didn't like chasing after people. For a minute, it was exciting, then it became annoying

CHAPTER 1

and dangerous. Jumping fences with a vest and duty belt on and then landing took a toll on my back and knees, not to mention the person I was chasing could stop, turn around, and shoot. A solution I learned was to have people just sit down. This simple request reduced the temptation to flee. They say policing is a young man's game, but the wisdom of maturity can reduce the risk to everyone—clearly a conundrum.

Instructors at the South Carolina Police Academy explained how people can be passive up until the time the handcuffs start to go on. I realized if I waited to assess the willingness of a person to comply with the order of "Turn around, you're under arrest," I was behind the curve. The fight or flight physiological response is an automatic reaction to perceiving a situation as either stressful or frightening. As a new law enforcement officer, I misconstrued this response as just a criminal trying to escape, or worse as an effort to do harm to me as a law enforcement officer. Recently, there has been an alarming increase in the latter, where police are called to scenes only to be ambushed. The unfortunate consequence of this could become more police acting quickly to use deadly force as their fight or flight response is propelled into overdrive.

Interrupting the fight or flight response is challenging, whether it's from the citizen who is being arrested or the law enforcement officer. I learned to recognize when to use a stronger officer presence or more calming language to disrupt the acute stress response in a citizen. People often show signs of impending resistance. Obvious signs like jaw clenching, balled up fists, and a defensive stance are easy to recognize, which allows time to step back and hopefully calm the situation or at least wait for more backup. But as they say, it's always the quiet ones who seem peaceful until the very last minute when they attack, leaving no time but to respond with force.

While I was waiting to be transferred to the Central Investigation Division (CID), I was approached by the sergeant in charge of the training division as well as the lead training deputy about being a Field Training Instructor (FTI). I agreed to be an FTI, and I then began to contemplate exactly how I would train a "rookie." Memories of the many lessons learned over the years emerged.

Dissecting my vocation is an interesting exercise which requires deep reflection into what it is I actually performed on a daily basis, situation by situation. After several trainees, I actually felt like I had a better understanding or at least a stronger insight into the intricacies of performing certain aspects of policing.

To illustrate, a "routine" traffic stop like the one mentioned above is not so routine. The process remains the same whether a traffic violation is observed first, or some other suspicious activity is initially observed. Probable cause must be established prior to the traffic stop. This could be an infraction of any number of traffic offenses, vehicle equipment issues, or other criminal offenses. Now, and this is the part where the race of the driver has become tremendously contentious, some will argue they were *only* stopped because of their race. My response is that the race, age, or gender is not always known. Especially at night and even during a bright sunny day, tinted windows obscure everything inside a vehicle like the number of passengers, let alone the race of the occupants. Do some police officers, after identifying the race of the driver, hunt for a violation as the basis for a traffic stop? Yes, they do. However, it cuts both ways, meaning any race can trigger a suspicion depending on the circumstances. A white person circling the block a few times late at night in a known drug area where coincidentally more minorities reside in that area could be suspicious, particularly if in the experience of the police officer this observation ended with a drug possession arrest more often than not. Although, these days most drug deals are not made on the corner. Drug dealers get text messages on burner phones and meet their customers at their house or some convenience store parking lot.

Once an officer identifies probable cause, there is a process to initiating a traffic stop. My process developed over time. I realized early on I had to have my script and general actions memorized and choreographed. The idea was to avoid consciously thinking about the mechanics of stopping a car and the initial

CHAPTER 1

verbal interaction, thus devoting most attention to any possible life and death threat.

When I started as an FTI I knew, subconsciously, I acted in a certain way in various circumstances, positioned myself for safety according to the situation, provided specific information to dispatch, and used all of my senses. How to convey, teach, and explain all of these internal and external factors to a trainee was the challenge. I did a lot of talking, asking questions and yelling to get my point across—a combination of drill sergeant and professor.

The mechanical aspects were fairly simple to explain. Don't stand with your back to the highway after asking the driver to exit the vehicle. Why? What if he just killed his wife and thinks you are onto him? One quick shove into traffic, and it becomes a bad day. Always be aware of your surroundings. You may be surprised by the number of things not previously noticed if you begin to concentrate and actively observe and listen.

Attitude, demeanor, volume, and tone are just as important as what is said but more difficult to instruct beyond explanation. Law enforcement officers, through their hostility, can cause immediate animosity, sending the scenario spinning out of control. Conversely, innocuous delivery of simple and genuine language can disarm even the most unfriendly. Sometimes it's not what you say but how you say it. This adage applies equally to both parties involved: police and citizen. (More on this in Chapter 9). Then sometimes... it's exactly *what* you say.

Occasionally, even seasoned police officers have trouble finding the right words, or the words they do find just aren't right.

Narcotics raid.

"Hey man, just relax back there. We'll be on our way as soon as the lieutenant says we can go." I had the main suspect of a drug raid in the back of my cruiser, waiting to take him to jail on a warrant for his arrest.

Handcuffed suspect said, "A'ight officer, I'm just worried about my moms."

Narcotics lieutenant opened the door, leaned into the car, and in a loud, laughing manner said, "I got you. I got you.

You're going to jail for so long your mama will be dead before you get out."

Did he just say what I think he said?

Suspect started bouncing up and down in the seat and slamming against the cage. "Oh no! No! No, you didn't fucking say that."

The lieutenant shut the door, still laughing.

The lieutenant was seemingly trying to inflict mental anguish upon the suspect for no other reason than deriving his own sadistic pleasure.

And there are other times where an officer recognizes an individual is clearly in distress and will most likely respond favorably to kind words spoken in a calm and sympathetic tone rather than harsh commands.

Naked guy Marion Square.

Foot patrol unit. "Control, a naked guy just ran from me. He is headed toward King and Calhoun."

"Control, we have the subject stopped by the fountain."

A tall, completely naked man grasped his genitals with one hand, pulling, and squeezing so hard they looked like a balloon ready to pop.

Naked man yelled, "Get it off me! It's trying to bite me."

The sergeant, 6'4" 250 pounds, former college offensive lineman, said in a calm soft tone, "It's okay, man. We're here to help you. We can protect you. Can you talk to these nice people with EMS?"

The naked man released his genitals. "Okay, sergeant. Thank you."

This simple act of kindness demonstrates that respect, courtesy, and empathy can resolve a tense situation in a positive way.

Since the advent of modern-day policing, the necessity of using force has been addressed. Sir Robert Peel, in 1829, established the Metropolitan Police in London. Peel set forth nine

CHAPTER 1

guiding principles. Two of the nine principles[2] (Moore, 2015) relevant to this discussion are as follows:
1. The degree of cooperation of the public that can be secured diminishes, proportionately, the necessity for

---

[2] The nine principles of policing developed by Sir Robert Peel:
- The basic mission for which police exist is to prevent crime and disorder as an alternative to the repression of crime and disorder by military force and severity of legal punishment.
- The ability of the police to perform their duties is dependent upon public approval of police existence, actions, behavior, and the ability of the police to secure and maintain public respect.
- The police must secure the willing cooperation of the public in voluntary observance of the law to be able to secure and maintain public respect.
- The degree of cooperation of the public that can be secured diminishes, proportionately, the necessity for the use of physical force and compulsion in achieving police objectives.
- The police seek and preserve public favor, not by catering to public opinion, but by constantly demonstrating absolutely impartial service to the law, in complete independence of policy, and without regard to the justice or injustice of the substance of individual laws; by ready offering of individual service and friendship to all members of the society without regard to their race or social standing; by ready exercise of courtesy and friendly good humor; and by ready offering of individual sacrifice in protecting and preserving life.
- The police should use physical force to the extent necessary to secure observance of the law or to restore order only when the exercise of persuasion, advice, and warning is found to be insufficient to achieve police objectives; and police should use only the minimum degree of physical force which is necessary on any particular occasion for achieving a police objective.
- The police at all times should maintain a relationship with the public that gives reality to the historic tradition that the police are the public, and that the public are the police; the police are the only members of the public who are paid to give full-time attention to duties which are incumbent on every citizen in the interest of the community welfare.
- The police should always direct their actions toward their functions and never appear to usurp the powers of the judiciary by avenging individuals or the state or authoritatively judging guilt or punishing the guilty.
- The test of police efficiency is the absence of crime and disorder, not the visible evidence of police action in dealing with them.

the use of physical force and compulsion in achieving police objectives.

2. The police should use physical force to the extent necessary to secure observance of the law or to restore order only when the exercise of persuasion, advice, and warning is found to be insufficient to achieve police objectives; and police should use only the minimum degree of physical force which is necessary on any particular occasion for achieving a police objective (Moore, 2015).

These principles were developed almost 200 years ago and still hold true today. However, cries of heavy-handed policing and brutality spawned the new doctrine of de-escalation. As mentioned in the prologue, de-escalation in operation has a fundamental flaw based on the initial situational premise, but I couldn't parse it out exactly until recently.

De-escalation within the last ten years has become the panacea to reducing the seemingly high number of police excessive use of force situations and police shootings of unarmed citizens.

Advocates pushed and continue to praise de-escalation training, arguing that citizens won't be safe until all officers in the country are certified in de-escalation. Isn't it interesting? A certification in treating people with dignity and respect. However, "experts who study de-escalation, as well as law enforcement officials who mandate it for their forces, say it's a mixed bag. On the one hand, there's no conclusive evidence that de-escalation training works. There's also no evidence that it doesn't work. And the training has never been rigorously studied at all" (Schumaker, 2020). Not exactly a ringing endorsement.

Police have been increasingly demonized since Rodney King was brutally beaten down on a Los Angeles street. Some criticisms are absolutely justified.

The exact same story at times receives vastly divergent headlines and reporting by the media. Case in point: Michael Brown.

CHAPTER 1

"Missouri cop was badly beaten before shooting Michael Brown, says source" (McKay, 2014).

"Missouri teen shot by police was two days away from starting college" (Shoichet, 2014).

So, there I was minding my own business in May of 2020, working from home. I was no longer in the policing game but still very much attuned to all the rhetoric. Another violent confrontation occurred between a citizen and several law enforcement officers. The George Floyd incident in Minneapolis was a horrible thing to watch. Little did I know it would touch off a firestorm of displayed hatred for all police and the call for dismantling policing as an institution.

More video of the Minneapolis incident began to emerge, and the media continued with talk of de-escalation. The fundamental flaw in the main situational premise was finally revealed to me. The implication of the word de-escalation alone suggests an unruly individual must be negotiated. After much thought, I realized de-escalation is like arriving late to the party when people are already swinging from the chandelier or dancing on the tables. If you have to de-escalate an encounter, it's already too late. A touch of humanity, the human element, is the missing link I finally identified after much reflection.

Today's society likes catch-phrases, one-liners, and clever terms. I searched for a word to capture the name for the mindset I was contemplating. Deconfliction was perfect. The thought process surrounds avoiding a conflict rather than learning how to lower the tenor, which seems like trying to put the toothpaste back into the tube.

Deconfliction and the Principles evolved into not only a way of structuring how police could externally approach citizens but a way to internally review how their own demeanor is outwardly perceived. Some of the behavior and psychological topic areas are, in fact, borrowed from de-escalation, but deconfliction goes beyond a progressive process that calls for acting in certain ways and instead focuses on thinking about ten different interactive Deconfliction Principles to peacefully resolve police-citizen interactions. Citizens could also employ the Deconfliction Principles.

A final note on the traffic stop and the cussing woman—a careless driving citation was issued rather than the four-point citation for disregarding a traffic control device. In court, she sincerely demonstrated a palpably different attitude and graciously apologized. I dismissed the citation.

CHAPTER 2

LAW ENFORCEMENT TRAINING STANDARDS

"266, dispatch. Traffic stop—Old Towne and Sumar."

"Dispatch, 266, go ahead with your traffic stop."

"Gray Buick, expired South Carolina tag, occupied three times. We'll be in the Publix parking lot."

"Copy."

"266, dispatch, the vehicle didn't stop and is heading over the North Bridge back into North Charleston. I'm in pursuit."

"Dispatch, copy."

"Dispatch, they just threw a gun out of the vehicle!"

This chase went on for another 15 to 20 minutes with the driver of the vehicle circling a neighborhood where all three lived. A proverbial parade of law enforcement vehicles from the Charleston County Sheriff's Office and North Charleston City

Police Department followed the vehicle as it rolled through the area until the driver finally stopped and gave up.

Once the parties were in custody, we discovered two of the occupants were juveniles and one barely an adult by one year. A North Charleston Officer told me the adult of the group was a suspect in multiple armed robberies in their jurisdiction. It seemed likely to me, considering a gun was tossed from the vehicle, that criminal activity was afoot or at least in contemplation.

Remember, the traffic stop was predicated on an expired registration[3], which, it has been suggested, should not serve as the basis for a traffic stop, let alone a pursuit. However, within minutes of the pursuit, a weapon was thrown from the vehicle, adding further probable cause. Furthermore, the happy trio was more than likely on their way to commit yet another armed robbery. I'm thinking they weren't so happy when I pulled behind them.

Law enforcement officers in South Carolina are trained in two methods of stopping a pursuit. The first is to continue the pursuit until the suspect vehicle stops, which really is not a method of stopping a pursuit. Second is the use of a tire deflation device which must be precariously placed into the path of the fleeing vehicle. Pursuits are dangerous, not only to the officer and suspect, but also to the innocent public. Many unsuspecting citizens who just happen to be in the wrong place at the wrong time have been severely injured and killed by fleeing suspects.

Florida's Pinellas County Sheriff's Office, where I briefly worked, is a very professional agency and is typically on the

---

[3] The first thing drawing my attention to the vehicle was the manner in which the driver was operating it. Namely, the driver was weaving in and out of traffic in what appeared to be a desire to put as much distance between us as possible. I then discovered through a computer check that the tag was expired and suspended, which can be an indication the operator's license is suspended, if the driver is the owner. It was only then did I observe that the rear passenger was a Black male. I was unable to see the gender or race of the two front passengers until the vehicle eventually stopped, and they exited the vehicle. My point here is that race was never a factor in deciding to initiate a traffic stop.

CHAPTER 2

cutting edge of training and technology. The Sheriff's Office training included the Pursuit Intervention Technique or (PIT). The philosophy of the Sheriff's Office is to end a pursuit quickly to reduce the danger to the public.[4]

States have specific requirements, standards, and training for police certification. The pursuit ending methods are but one difference between agencies and states. South Carolina, in 2002, required 9 weeks of academy training consisting of classroom legal instruction, firearms training, defensive tactics, first responder first aid, and emergency driving operations. Currently, the training in South Carolina is 12 weeks compared to 28 weeks in Pennsylvania, 35 weeks for Virginia State Troopers, 20 weeks for Massachusetts police, 18 weeks in Texas, and 24 weeks in California. Obviously, a great disparity exists across the country in the length of police academy training. Some states also allow newly hired officers to work as a patrol officer for a number of months before being required to attend an academy. There are currently 37 states which don't require academy training for new recruits before they start working (The Institute for Criminal Justice Training Reform, n.d.).

Additionally, on average, only a week or 40 hours are devoted to scenario-based training at academies across the country. Realism in training is also an issue along with instilling some muscle memory, which could lead to reaction without full mental processing.

---

[4] The PIT maneuver is based upon Newton's first law of motion: a body in motion at a constant velocity will remain in motion in a straight line unless acted upon it by an outside force. The PIT requires a slight nudge of the rear quarter panel of the fleeing vehicle, thus causing the backend of the vehicle to change direction, lose traction, and cause a spin out. Pinellas County Sheriff's Office taught to only use the PIT on a vehicle traveling less than 50mph to reduce potential collision with other vehicles or objects. Additionally, the PIT was not to be used on trucks or Sport Utility Vehicles as they tended to roll over. These protocols, however, are not followed across the country as evidenced by many videos showing very high-speed PIT applications ending in tragedy. Moreover, a deadly force situation, like the suspect shooting from the moving vehicle, incurs a flexibility of policies.

Field training is the final preparation for a new officer. Rookies, as they are affectionately called, are evaluated by a field training officer and taught how each individual department operates.

The amount of time in field training also varies across the country from 12 to 18 weeks. An exceptional training officer will impart years of knowledge to a "rookie," focusing on lessons that will keep inexperienced officers safe.

There are no national standards regulating how police perform their job; however, there are standards related to law enforcement agency accreditation, which, de facto, correlates policies and procedures across all certified organizations. The largest national accreditation organization is the Commission on Accreditation for Law Enforcement Agencies (CALEA).[5] The accreditation process seeks to provide a level of consistency across the nation regarding the language contained within police policies.

Below is an example of a CALEA standard related to the use of reasonable force (revised 6/22/22):

Officers shall use reasonable care when determining whether and when to use physical force against another. Officers shall use only that amount of force that reasonably appears necessary given the facts and circumstances perceived by the officer at the time of the event to accomplish a legitimate law enforcement purpose. To that end, officers shall:

1. De-Escalate. When feasible, use all de-escalation tactics that are available and appropriate under the circumstances before using physical force (Bell PD, 2022).

In the previous chapter, footnote two set forth the nine principles of policing developed by Sir Robert Peel. The reference above reduces one of the Peel principles to a basic premise. The idea of using only reasonable force necessary to achieve lawful

---

[5] A comprehensive list of standard titles in the Law Enforcement Standards Manual 6th edition can be found at: https://www.calea.org/node/11406.

CHAPTER 2

objectives is the "what," "when," and "why" of problem solving. The "how" is left open for interpretation of application. The use of force continuum, which is explained in greater detail in the next chapter, attempts to codify the "how." Although, even when applying the force continuum to a real-life situation, in recent times there has been much condemnation of actions.

An instance of this scrutiny occurred in Columbus, Ohio, in April of 2021. Police were called to a disturbance, and the first officer on scene encountered a chaotic group of individuals yelling and screaming in the driveway. A young female attacked another female in front of the officer. The same young female attacker then lunged for another female juvenile with a knife. The officer observed the knife and drew his firearm and milliseconds before the girl with the knife stabbed the juvenile, the officer shot her. Unfortunately, the officer had to take a life to save a life. The situation escalated quickly, which forced the officer to make a split-second decision.

The use of force continuum allows for the use of deadly force to confront deadly force. After the tragic situation in Ohio, there was an immediate outcry from some journalists blaming the incident on racism followed up by uninformed statements like, "How do I teach my daughters when you call for help, and you expect help to come, you could be on the other side of the gun?" (Vigdor & Pietsch, 2021). Even after it was revealed from the police body camera footage how the deceased girl had a knife and was attempting to stab another girl, people suggested more training could have changed the outcome. A law enforcement expert suggested police are "trained to consider if they should use force" (Crisp, 2021). I respectfully disagree. Police are trained to consider factors like imminent physical harm to their own person or bystanders when reacting to a quickly developing situation. The key term is reacting. Police are taught to react to an ongoing situation in an instant with a level of force one degree above the resistance or aggressive behavior of an individual. Reacting is not considering.

A call for national standards for policing sounds like a solution to a perceived national problem. However, having the same standards in policing in Nome, Alaska, does not stop an instance of excessive use of force in Miami, Florida. The use of force policies in one state may not be acceptable politically or a tolerable liability in a different state. Standards should be left up to state legislators and law enforcement in consultation with the community. Additionally, federal guidelines for policing may seem heavy handed in one city and yet not be effective in addressing criminal activity in another.

Perhaps Congress could pass a federal law mandating the number of hours of training states must provide new police recruits with respect to the "high liability" areas as they are designated in Florida. Those areas are driving, shooting, first aid, and defensive tactics. Furthermore, Deconfliction training, which is outlined later in this book, could be mandated through federal legislation and tied to federal funding pursuant to Congress's spending powers enumerated in the Constitution. Currently, 21 states do not require de-escalation training for police (Stockton, 2021).

Additionally, federal legislation could require psychological testing beyond the usual assessments during the police hiring process. Police applicants, in most states, are subject to screening, "not to identify mentally ill applicants and 'psychos'— no police department has the resources to conduct such medically in-depth and costly assessments—but to flag prospective officers who may perform poorly in a high-stress profession that requires quick decision-making, emotional control, sound judgment in dangerous situations, honesty, teamwork, and strong communications" (El-Hai, 2016). However, according to El-Hai, "Some 20 states still fail to require psychological screening, evaluations are inconsistently conducted, and many smaller police forces forego the screenings entirely" (2016).

The long-term benefits of a recurring psychological review of an officer incorporating the actual performance statistics of the individual officer, although costly, could be immeasurable. A consistent assessment of the mental health, attitudes toward job satisfaction, and biases and possible racial animus of officers

CHAPTER 2

could uncover potential bad apples. Excessive use of force tendencies could also be revealed during these evaluations.

To illustrate the mental health issue above, the following is an example from my own experience. I will call him Trainee M, who could have benefited from ongoing psychological testing. Before he was assigned to me, another FTI recognized potential racial biases. Trainee M didn't talk much or reveal any personal information to me until he thought it would produce better evaluations. He was socially awkward and lacked the ability to communicate effectively with diverse types of people. He believed my instructions and criticisms were racially motivated. The situation culminated in trainee M wanting to go play with some kids, who were throwing around a football, when he hadn't even initiated one traffic stop all day. I told him no, he should do his job, and his career had not reached that level yet. He left the area then minutes later returned.

"Are you going back to where those kids are?" I asked in disbelief.

"Yes."

"Trainee M, pull the car over right now," I said in a stern tone while pointing to the side of the road.

"Sir, sir, you don't need to threaten me."

"M, pull the car over now and get out."

Trainee M stopped the cruiser, got out, and stood on the sidewalk.

"Trainee M, get in the car."

"Sir, no. I'm scared. I'll take an Uber back to headquarters."

I laughed. "Trainee M, I'm your FTI, and I am ordering you to get into the car. I am taking you back to headquarters."

Trainee M demonstrated other erratic and unpredictable behavior throughout his time with me such as admitting to me he only asked me personal questions to try and receive better scores on his evaluation. There was another time while we were on a medical call that Trainee M unexpectedly sat down in the middle of the road complaining that his knees were sore from standing.

Trainee M was transferred to another FTI after a few days off. The first night with the new FTI, trainee M put on his uniform, boots, and gun belt, and he waited at the station to start the shift. When the FTI arrived, trainee M quit and went back home.

More extensive psychological testing of potential law enforcement officers could uncover unstable individuals who may not be the best fit for the job.

As noted above, field training is another area which is not always standardized. However, when I was a field training instructor (FTI) with the Charleston County Sheriff's Office, I was required to complete a Daily Observation Report (DOR) for trainees. The DOR used by the Sheriff's Office contained 31 areas to evaluate if they applied. The first seven of the areas accessed were considered critical performance tasks: driving skill, orientation, and field performance under stressful conditions; officer safety in general and when in contact with suspicious persons or prisoners; and controlling conflict with voice command and physical skill if necessary. What was not standardized were the nuances of executing those critical performance areas. This is where an experienced FTI plays a key role in the final training of a new law enforcement officer.

During field training, the FTI or Field Training Officer (FTO) gives context to general academy training. An experienced FTI plays a critical role in the development of a well- rounded, fair, respectful, and professional law enforcement officer.

Conversely, an inexperienced FTI or an overly aggressive FTI can influence a trainee to become more forceful without considering all options when confronting a citizen. Deconfliction and the Deconfliction Principles, which are explained in detail in chapter 4, could go a long way toward counteracting undesirable traits, learned or innate, in a police officer.

An FTI who is overly passive in their approach to citizen interactions could impart the same docile approach to a trainee, thereby endangering the trainee as well as a citizen in contact with the officer. This idea may sound counterintuitive. Citizens can become violent when they are about to be arrested, and they know they are going to jail. A firm but polite approach by

CHAPTER 2

a law enforcement officer can quell a violent reaction to being arrested. In my opinion, in the current climate, much of the violence and criminal behavior has been personified by the lack of respect for any authority manifesting in defiance and the inability to appreciate consequences of actions since penalties and prosecutions have been abandoned by many jurisdictions. The topic of various catalysts increasing the defiance toward law enforcement is far beyond the scope of this book.

The preceding explanation regarding the underlying cause of criminal behavior relates to a broad spectrum. When in contact with an individual citizen possibly involved in criminal activity, the ultimate reason why someone is committing a crime is less important. What is important is a positive outcome for the officer and citizen. Fight or flight is a very real sympathetic nervous system response to being placed under arrest. It is way past the reason why someone has made the decision to commit a crime when they are being placed into handcuffs.

An officer who is aware of this natural psychological response to fight or flee can influence the coming reaction by the suspect with assertive commands and advantageous positioning like having someone sit on the ground as mentioned in the previous chapter. If a trainee adopts the passive nature of their FTI, they could inadvertently encourage arrestee resistance, which could lead to another unwanted police citizen encounter statistic. A law enforcement officer must strike a balance between assertive and passive to avoid any violent action by a citizen during arrest.

To illustrate this point, let's review the first portion of the incident in Brooklyn Center, Minnesota, where the police-citizen encounter ended with an African-American man losing his life.

The young man was pulled over by police for an expired license plate registration, and a routine driver's license check revealed a warrant for failing to appear for the charges of possession of a pistol without a permit and fleeing a police officer. The criminal charge would be significant information as police must assume all individuals could be armed, especially those who have demonstrated this behavior on previous occasions. The officer who attempted to place the subject into handcuffs was an officer in training. If you watch his actions in the video closely, you can conclude he was attempting to place the subject into custody in a very passive manner. If the young man had complied, the incident would have ended without any discussion. Even if there was a review, the arrest would have been seen as "humane" and "respectful," and frankly, it would have gone unreported. Unfortunately, hoping for the best outcome is not always the greatest approach. The officer in training provided an opportunity for the subject to act on emotion, and his fight or flight response replaced rational thought (Deliso, 2021).

I am not blaming the officer in training nor the young man for the ultimate outcome. The young man was acting out of fear of going to jail, and the officer in training was inexperienced. The duty of a citizen who is in contact with the police will be discussed in a later chapter as well as the actions which ultimately led to the death of the young man.

Officers must balance the use of force with the outcry which comes from lack of understanding about alleged overuse of force. The situation in Minnesota may have ended differently if the officer in training had taken hold of the subject firmly and moved him to the rear of the stopped vehicle. Would the subject's fight or flight response have been interrupted by moving him, causing him to comply? For the sake of argument, even if the subject decided to resist being placed into handcuffs, standing at the rear of the vehicle, his options would have been limited. The other officers on the scene could have reasonably thought there might be a gun in the car when the subject fought to get back into the vehicle. Sometimes, an officer must take the assertive road to avoid a more violent destination.

I trained 15 new Charleston County Deputies within 18 months as a field training instructor. Two of those deputies did have a few years of experience with other local agencies. Part of my training method consisted of trainer-induced stress. In my opinion, it was far better for me to rattle the nerves of a trainee to assess how they reacted to the pressure than for a citizen to test them. With this manner of training, I was able to understand the strengths and weaknesses of the trainee in a more controlled environment.

What kinds of stressors? Drill sergeants yell at basic trainees for a reason. Lessons include officer safety, which revolve around faster decision making and actions and staying "switched on" to remain aware of the surroundings, better known as situational awareness.

To drive a point home, sometimes I castigate my trainees with the harsh reality of policing. Here is but one example.

Trainee R said, "I'm going to stop and talk to that guy walking along the highway."

I, the FTI, said, "Alright, just do it safely."

It was night shift, and the area was completely dark on a four-lane highway with no streetlights. Only the headlights of the numerous cars passing illuminated the area. Trainee R completed a series of U-turns and notified dispatch she was getting out with a pedestrian but failed to give a description of the individual and precise location of the stop. She pulled off the roadway with the pedestrian behind the patrol vehicle. I did not get out of the vehicle. I wanted her to get a sense of being all alone, in the dark, with this man on the side of a busy road. She stood with her back to traffic during the encounter. She never asked him for identification, nor did she ask dispatch to check for warrants. Yes, it was reasonable for trainee R to stop and talk to the individual.[6]

---

[6] An officer is free to approach anyone and talk to them. It is not a violation of any rights for an officer to ask someone who they are and what they are doing. It is also the right of an individual to refuse to talk to the officer and walk away. If the officer cannot articulate any reasonable suspicion (belief a person is committing or about to commit a crime) or probable cause (reasonable belief a crime has been committed, and a particular person has committed the crime), then it is not lawful for the officer to detain the person and ask for identification. However, along with asking who someone is and what they are doing, an officer is free to ask if someone has identification. Absent reasonable suspicion or probable cause, an officer demanding to see identification would be violating the person's civil rights.

A few minutes later, she returned to the cruiser. I didn't say a word until I asked, "So how do you think that went?"

"I think it went fine. How would you have handled it? If you would have even stopped to check on him?"

She was implying I was heartless and didn't care if he needed assistance. She portrayed an attitude that she was young and respected people better than older officers, and she was out to prove how nice officers could be to citizens.

My response in a forceful tone was, "Well, first I would have stopped so he was in front of the car so I could use the lights to see him and use the camera. Then I would not have stood with my back to the road because if he wanted to, he could have shoved you in front of a passing car, and I would have checked him for warrants. I don't care if you want to save everyone. Just do it safely because I don't want to go to your fucking funeral."

The patrol car was extraordinarily quiet the rest of the shift.

I was hoping that Trainee R would heed my words and one day that jarring admonishment would keep her safe.

To foster more uniform policing across the country, national standards for training could either be a panacea for excessive use of force or a response with no substance. Standards focusing on micro responses to specific situations would make an already difficult job downright impossible. Broad spectrum standards could seem beneficial; however, this may only add to the cost of training law enforcement officers and completely miss the intended goal.

The definitive goal is to hire well-suited recruits, train them effectively and efficiently to reduce instances of excessive use of force, make the community a safer place, and improve police citizen interactions.

CHAPTER 3

REALITIES OF TRAINING

"266, 94. Respond to assist EMS with a combative white male who has a deep laceration to the foot."

"Both units copy."

It was after 4:00 p.m. when the call came in. Jason and I were sitting in a parking lot talking, waiting for our shift to end at 6:00 p.m.

When we arrived on scene, EMS was there along with the Fire Department, and the patient was standing on his front porch yelling at everyone.

"I don't need fucking help. Leave me the fuck alone."

This is just stupid.

The patient was in his late 20s, intoxicated and bleeding severely from his foot after stepping on a broken bottle. He refused all help. His father, who called 911, indicated his son may be on drugs, just recently was shot, and now had a colostomy bag.[7]

The patient would occasionally walk out onto the front porch, yell obscenities at us, telling us to leave him the "fuck" alone, and then go back into the house. The alcohol in his system was not allowing his blood to clot, so he was bleeding absolutely everywhere.

I assumed the contact officer role, and Jason was the cover officer, which was ironic thinking about it later since Jason had extensive negotiator training. I was respectful and politely asked him to allow EMS to look at his foot since he seemed to have lost so much blood. I told the patient his father was concerned for his well-being as all of us were, and we just wanted him to get help.

I want to help this dude, but honestly, I just want him to get in the ambulance so I can go home on time.

This scene went on for at least 20 minutes. The patient stood on the front porch, and if we tried to get close, he would run back inside the house.

His girlfriend arrived at the house with their daughter, and we asked her if she could try and talk him into going with EMS. The daughter was 8 to 10 years old. This quickly turned into a huge error.

The girlfriend opened the front door with the daughter standing next to her. In an instant, the patient ushered both inside the house and closed the door. Jason and I looked at each other, and he let out a short laugh.

"Fuck." The situation just went from bad to worse.

A few minutes later, the patient again opened the door and stood on the porch yelling at us, but this time, he had a large bandage on his foot. There was so much blood it would not stay attached even for a second. As he performed this

---

[7] We found out later a Charleston City Police narcotics officer was conducting surveillance on the patient during the incident. The narco guy told us the patient was a drug dealer and had been shot a few weeks earlier in a drug robbery—all useful information, which would have been nice to know at the start of the incident.

CHAPTER 3

dramatic gesture, his daughter stepped out of the house and stood next to him. He reached down with his hand full of blood and touched her head, guiding her back into the house before slamming the door.

We need a different tactic.[8]

This situation is a fitting example of the extent to which the use of force continuum could become challenging. The typical "use of force" continuum model is presented to law enforcement officers as a matrix with levels of resistance with correlating levels of force (See Figure 1). However, "the concept of the continuum was to explain to officers 'when' to use force options as opposed to the traditional defensive tactics class which dealt only with 'how' to use force options. Thus, the continuum was designed to be a training tool" (Marker, 2012).

The force continuum, as suggested above, is a guide or training tool for using the appropriate force. Issues can arise when an officer steadfastly follows the force continuum in the prescribed, sometimes unrealistic, order. Actions on the surface may falsely or not completely reveal the true threat the individual poses.

Use-of-force continuum images challenge effective decision-making by officers. Use-of-force continuum images present

---

[8] The different tactic included Jason standing off to the side obscured by a bush with his Taser at the ready. Then, instead of pleading with the guy, I unleashed a barrage of insults, calling him the dumbest motherfucker I have ever met and daring him to put up or shut up. The idea was to challenge his pride so he would step forward to protect his masculinity. He responded as intended, moving farther toward the edge of the porch and close enough for Jason to emerge from the shadows and deploy his Taser. Just prior to being struck with the probes from the Taser, the patient pulled his colostomy bag off and attempted to throw it at us; however, Jason was too quick and just dropped the bag on the porch. The patient fell backward like a tree falling in the woods but then was able to crawl back into the house and tried to shut the door. Jason and I pushed on the door as we stepped around the blood and spilled contents of the colostomy bag. I was able to reach inside the door and, for the first time ever, deployed my Taser. The patient eventually complied, and I was able to place handcuffs on him. EMS moved in, hoisted him onto the gurney, and transported him to the hospital.

an overly simplistic approach to decision-making that detracts from the officer's ability to make effective decisions when confronted by resistance in real time. Departments should encourage officers through contemporary policies and training to evaluate the situation with decision-making methods, such as proper tactics, communication skills, and de-escalation tactics, rather than a stair-stepping methodology (Daigle Law Group, 2020).

The levels of control, as shown in figure 1, are potentially misleading. It must be remembered that law enforcement officers are taught various techniques contained within each level of control; however, the level of force used in a specific situation is dictated by the actions of the citizen in contact with the officer. Therefore, levels of control in practice are defensive and reactive in nature.

Levels of Resistance or Threat	Cooperative	Verbal & Nonverbal Noncompliance	Passive Resistance	Defensive Resistance	Active Resistance	Active Aggression	Aggravated Active Aggression
Levels of Control	Professional Police Presence						
	Verbal Dialogue and Direction						
			Soft Empty Hand Control				
				Hard Empty Hand Control			
					OC Spray/Chemical Agents		
					Conducted Electrical Weapon		
						Impact Weapons	
							Lethal Force

Figure 1 From the Greenville, SC (Greenville, SC Police Department General Order, 2020)

Police are taught to match the resistance or threat level encountered, plus one level up, if needed to stabilize the situation. The use of force is not a mechanical application of the force continuum but a fluid process which can evolve rapidly. Defensive tactics are always one step behind the resistance of the aggressor. Reaction is slower than action.

By example, a real-world scenario:

CHAPTER 3

Market Street in Charleston, South Carolina, is always busy and even more so on a hot and steamy weekend night. Shopping market by day, restaurant and bar by evening, the scene transforms into a wild, fun, alive with excitement area. For the most part orderly, the area is disciplined in part due to the number of on- and off-duty police officers watching for the first sign of mischief, calamity, or buffoonery.

On one such evening, I was on duty and stopped to talk to a few officers working off duty for two separate bars: a martini bar on the first floor and an upstairs place where the pretty girls wearing jean shorts danced on the bar.

We heard shouting coming from the stairwell leading up to the girls dancing on the bar establishment. Another officer (Will) and I stepped into the doorway, and halfway up the stairs, we saw a very muscular man shouting back at several bouncers who were standing at the top of the stairwell yelling for the man to leave.

Officer presence is the first level of control, and stepping into the doorway announced our presence without saying a word; thus, the force continuum began. Revealing ourselves immediately escalated the situation and instantly involved the concept of de-escalation. A law enforcement officer by virtue of being on scene and recognized as law enforcement escalates the situation. There is no way to avoid this.

Next, verbal commands can further intensify a situation, and how an officer delivers those commands can determine if the citizen will comply or not comply. Deconfliction attempts to produce more compliance than non-compliance. De-escalation, which continues to be sold as the answer to reducing deadly police citizen encounters, is similar to capturing a swarm of bees with a shotgun. When the heat of a situation rises to the level where de-escalation techniques are needed, it's more likely a physical altercation will be the outcome.

De-escalation techniques, to be sure, at times are necessary; however, the use-of-force continuum and de-escalation are at odds and the premise of each are diametrically opposed.

De-escalation prescribes lowering the temperature, whereas the force continuum dictates an elevation.

Deconfliction seeks to create a positive atmosphere even prior to direct police-citizen contact, thereby avoiding both de-escalation and the need for additional force.

"De-escalation is a broad term," explained Chuck Wexler, executive director of the nonprofit Police Executive Research Forum, an organization focused on improving policing.

Traditional policing often escalates tense situations involving civilians, according to Wexler. "'A person has a rock. They take out a baton,' Wexler said" (Schumaker, 2020).

De-escalation is used to slow the tempo down. Deconfliction, in contrast, attempts to humanize police-citizen interactions. De-escalation focuses on the actions of an officer in relation to the citizen. Deconfliction centers on the attitudes of the law enforcement officer before contact is initiated.

Wexler highlighted a few of the de-escalation strategies offered during training by numerous agencies:

- Listen respectfully. Don't argue or interrupt. Many times, angry people calm down when they feel they've been listened to and taken seriously. Make sure that each person in the conflict has a chance to talk.

- Don't allow an audience to gather. If two people are having an argument, isolate them from friends or family members. Removing a potential audience sometimes eliminates the need to show off with angry and aggressive behavior.

- Set an example. Use courteous, professional language to convey the message that talk must be calm and respectful.

- Be aware of body language. Don't point or jab a finger at a citizen. Don't loom over anyone.

- Maintain control. Cut off offensive speech (cursing, yelling, insults) by asking the person to restate the point in acceptable language.

- Don't publicly humiliate anyone—especially when others are watching. If you have to perform a pat down or ask potentially embarrassing questions, take the person aside.

- Remember that the only person whose behavior and thinking you can absolutely control is you. Don't waste time and energy trying to convince a citizen that he's wrong and you're right. Do what you need to do (such as writing a citation or making an arrest) without becoming defensive.

- Remember that "broken record" is a useful way to achieve two goals—conveying the message that you're in charge while keeping the lid on a potential conflict. "Broken record" means repeating a message as many times as needed: "I'm writing a citation. You'll have an opportunity to state your case in court." If a citizen argues, you refuse to take the bait. You simply repeat your message until the citation is written, and your job is done.

De-escalating a police conflict takes brains, training, and practice. If you're offered a chance to attend a de-escalation training session, take it seriously. The strategies you'll be learning could save a life someday—possibly your own (Reynolds, 2019 and Wexler, 2016).

Sometimes, de-escalation is not possible. Back at the stairwell in Charleston, Will and I practiced the de-escalation techniques discussed above by listening respectfully, setting the example by being courteous, and not publicly humiliating the muscle-bound man.[9] The one thing we did, which may have

---

[9] It must be noted that this situation occurred in the early 2000s when de-escalation was not widely trained. It wasn't until about 2016 when de-escalation training began to emerge.

been the catalyst, was hold onto the muscle man's arms. I had his left arm and Will the other. We were politely escorting him from the stairwell and out the front door. He may have thought he was going to jail, or maybe he didn't like how we were holding onto him. As Will and I reached the bottom of the stairs, the muscle man started to toss us to-and-fro like rag dolls and yelled, "Is that all you got?" The situation quickly turned into a four-on-one all out brawl with Will, two other officers, and me. We were losing for the first few minutes.

Well, this is not going like I thought it would.

Will was able to get behind the muscle man as the other two officers joined in, trying to subdue the man. Will pulled the man backward and down to the floor. After a few more minutes of a struggle, we were able to handcuff the man who continued to curse as we placed him into the back of my cruiser. When I reached the station, I opened the car door and politely told the man the football game was over, and if he cooperated, I would work with him on the charges. The very muscular man looked up at me and, with tears streaming down his face, cried out, "I'm a real estate agent."

Oh, good lord, we have a crier.

The muscle man incident is a classic example of how even when law enforcement officers attempt to forestall a violent encounter the situation can turn in an instant. If we had approached the situation heavy handed from the start it would have been more likely to end with an altercation; however, you just never know.

Experience builds upon training, but training lays the foundation for more professional policing. Police academies across the country typically include the following areas in their curriculum: driving, shooting, first aid, defensive tactics, and of course criminal law. When I attended the police academy in South Carolina in 2002, it included only a week of practical applications of the law and tactics in various situations. The week of practical applications was more about controlling the situation through officer presence all the way to defensive tactics. Police learn at the academy, as well as on the street, to vocalize the

CHAPTER 3

phrase "Stop resisting," which is not necessarily directed at the suspect, but more to notify the citizens who may be observing the arrest how the suspect is, in fact, resisting.

As a field training instructor, the first thing I taught new trainees was to always know their legal right for being where they were and their legal right for what they were doing. In other words, they could always recognize if the legal ground they were standing on was firm.

With regard to tactics, I always stressed considering all possible threats and being completely aware of the surroundings by using all of the senses. I did notice several unfortunate trends with younger recruits such as the inability to verbally interact with people eye-to-eye and the propensity to mentally shut down when criticized. We can debate why this behavior is more prevalent in younger individuals, but we can save it for another time and place. What is important to take away from this observation is that police must be able to ignore direct personal attacks to maintain their vigilance and professionalism.

My opinion, through observations of recent rhetoric, is that citizens have an unrealistic expectation of police psychological capabilities. Fear is real, even for law enforcement officers. There are more reasons to be on edge as a law enforcement officer in these times as respect for authority has diminished and has been replaced with targeting officers.

It takes time and experience to learn how to control fear, and adrenaline floods through an officer's veins as they charge into a dangerous situation, knowing life and death may be in the balance. Sound dramatic? It's not. It is reality. I have been there firsthand. I was fortunate to have prior experience involving stressful and intense situations before I began my law enforcement career.

"Foot pursuit!"

Within the first few years of my career with the Charleston City Police, I engaged in multiple foot chases. I worked in a high drug area where dealers still sold dope on the corner. The other officer I was working with had more experience, and he was aggressive and very proactive. It was night, and we approached several individuals congregating in a baseball field. This type of activity was common for people selling and buying various narcotics in the area; thus, it served as our reasonable suspicion to approach them to find out what they were doing.

As we approached, they all took off running in different directions. I chased after one guy who fled across a busy highway without even slowing down to look. I, on the other hand, had to stop for traffic or risk being run down by a passing motorist. The guy disappeared into a small wooded lot on the other side of the highway.

When you chase someone and you lose sight of them, it's prudent to slow down and search slowly. It's better to let the person abscond than to be ambushed.

I worked my way through a small worn path in the wood line when my flashlight lit up the guy laying on the ground. I ordered him to not move[10], which can be the safest for everyone. However, he did not comply. After getting to his feet, the young man walked quickly toward me as I pointed my Glock 21 (45cal) handgun at him, ordering him to stop. He kept coming, and I did not observe any weapon in his hands, so the Glock was useless. The solution to the situation came in the form of a quick front kick to the abdomen, causing him to double over. Afterward, it was pretty easy to place him on the ground and quickly handcuff him. This incident could have ended very differently if I were someone who scared easily.

Most individuals who gravitate toward law enforcement have type "A" personalities. Young recruits, working with proactive officers, can be influenced into getting "into the shit." This can be disastrous if a virgin officer has not learned how to

---

[10] I have personally heard some officers yell, "Let me see your hands" to people they are attempting to detain. I also know of one real-life situation where the law enforcement officer yelled, "Let me see your hands," and less than a second later shot the individual, who was holding a gun in his hand; however, he was a resident of the house who just chased off a home invader. I don't recall being taught in the academy to command someone to show me their hands. Although, I don't recall being taught to not to use the command either.

CHAPTER 3

control and channel their fear-driven aggression or plain old aggression.

The rhetoric after a police shooting is many times unrealistic. Take the following uttered by an infamous politician: "Instead of anybody coming at you and the first thing you do is shoot to kill, you shoot them in the leg."[11] Even the best police marksman would have a difficult time, under stressful conditions with the suspect moving, hitting a relatively small target like a leg. Not to mention a very large blood vessel commonly referred to as the femoral artery runs along the upper thigh, and a person could die from exsanguination in a matter of seconds (Blavias, Shiver, & Adhikari, 2006).

This type of comment along with other statements seemingly gives the impression that police officers in general are akin to a member of SEAL Team Six or an elite Delta Force operator.[12] Only the best, mature, and experienced individuals ever make it to the Army Delta Team. They are bad asses and can remain calm under the highest combat stress conditions. It's a fallacy to think the majority of police are trained and experienced at this level.

Most law enforcement officers are not hardened combat veterans. This is a concept overlooked when scrutinizing police actions with regard to the application of force.

---

[11] Statement made by Joe Biden during the 2020 presidential campaign at an ABC News town hall.

[12] Delta Force is primarily a tier-one counterterrorism unit, specifically directed to kill or capture high-value units or dismantle terrorist cells. Delta Force remains extremely flexible and can engage in direct-action missions, hostage rescues, and covert missions working directly with the CIA, as well as high-ranking protective services of our senior leaders during visits in war-torn countries (Smith, 2012).

However, a Supreme Court case[13] did attempt to put this concept into perspective. Unfortunately, the court only addressed looking at the facts at the time of the incident in a reasonable manner. The court did not opine about what constitutes a reasonable or average police officer. Moreover, the court did not include a parameter for looking at the experience level, maturity, and other mental factors of the officer under review. This perhaps would be too subjective, and the courts like objective standards.

Unfortunately, the objective reasonableness standard of judging the use of force seems to have gone by the wayside, and now excessive force is determined by individuals who are sitting in a comfortable chair in an air-conditioned office. One of the first factors considered is whether the officer attempted to de-escalate the situation. It appears now there is increased liability for officers and agencies if an officer does not attempt any de-escalation before using force up to and including lethal force. The situation may not have afforded the opportunity to do so, but like other second guessing, it could be extended to a time where an officer, in their reasonable judgement, did not have the time to talk the subject down.

An often-missed fact is the subject playing a role in the force an officer ultimately uses.

This does not mean de-escalation training should not be required, but there is a danger and potential of unintended consequence from mandatory training. This is where, in my view, Deconfliction training could be useful as it attempts to

---

[13] The Supreme Court case, Graham v Connor 490 U.S. 386 (1989) provided the framework for reviewing police use of force. "Under Graham, the government must weigh the need for force against the impact of force on the subject, and in so doing establish a compelling governmental interest for the intrusion. Under this guidance, Graham held the 'split-second' decision making required of police officers takes precedent over the benefit of hindsight. Force is to be judged from the reasonable observations of the facts as they presented themselves at the time force was applied; as such, Graham gives deference to the reasonable assumptions of the officer over facts as they may appear later. The objective reasonableness standard has come to be the prevailing method for analysis of force" (Atherley & Hickman, 2016).

CHAPTER 3

prevent a situation from progressing to the point where de-escalation becomes necessary. However, I would acknowledge the same argument of liability could be relevant if Deconfliction is not utilized.

In contrast to the de-escalation strategies listed above, the Deconfliction Principles incorporate the following:

1. Situational Awareness
2. Use Your Words
3. Active Listening
4. Empathy
5. Find Common Ground
6. Acknowledge the Problem
7. Confront Negative Feelings
8. Encourage Compromise
9. Be Positive
10. Give Choices

There is a dichotomy or maybe synergy between the Deconfliction Principles and the display of authority. Training for the use of force is designed to keep officers safe and take the suspect into custody with the least amount of force necessary and without injury to the suspect. With the emergence of "I can do what I want because I know my rights and cops are evil," resistance has outpaced the least amount of force necessary to effect an arrest. Deconfliction may not be the perfect solution, but it could ease tensions in certain situations before emotions take over during a police-citizen encounter.

CHAPTER 4

DECONFLICTION PRINCIPLES

"Dispatch, 266."

"266, respond to a combative female fighting with her mother and sister."

"Copy."

This type of call is played out multiple times a day throughout every jurisdiction in the country. In the incidents where police are shot and killed, the majority of those situations involve an aggressive individual either attempting to avoid arrest or out to kill a police officer. Alternatively, police interactions ending in a deceased citizen can involve emotionally charged circumstances, the mentally ill, mind-altering substance use, a belief in discriminatory attacks, or a combination thereof.

The difference between a positive outcome and a tragic one relies on how a law enforcement officer approaches and interacts with the citizen.

"266, dispatch, on scene."

Ashley, a 13-year-old-girl, locked herself in her bedroom and was heard throwing items around the room. The mother, who seemed to have mental issues of her own, spoke nothing but venom about Ashley while praising her younger daughter. Ashley had anger issues, the source of which I quickly identified after only a few minutes with the mother. I stood in the hallway outside Ashley's bedroom, contemplating my next move.

Ashley needed to have a psychological evaluation to determine if she was a risk to herself or others before we could take her into emergency protective custody (EPC). But first, she had to open the door.

The story of Ashley illustrates Deconfliction at work in its entirety. Deconfliction is different from de-escalation in that it is not a set of control strategies used to slow the tempo of a situation which is intensifying. Deconfliction is a manner of thinking, a mindset that can avoid or lessen the potential of conflict. Deconfliction focuses on mental and emotional considerations applied together in an attempt to enter the situation in a calm state and remain at that level throughout the police citizen interaction without having to resort to any de-escalation.

There are 10 principles within the Deconfliction framework, which are not applied in any specific order. All Deconfliction Principles should be considered and practiced with every police-citizen interaction and not only by the law enforcement officer but by citizens as well, a topic which will be discussed in a later chapter.

Within each Deconfliction Principle, there are elements defining the principle. For example, telling someone to be situationally aware is not truly explaining the concept.

Describing what actions comprise awareness goes further toward understanding the mindset needed to utilize Deconfliction and its Principles.

Deconfliction may seem simplistic on its face, which as a general concept, it is. However, Deconfliction is not a procedural process whereby "if this happens then employ this technique." As previously mentioned, it is a mindset requiring self-reflection and self-awareness of interpersonal communication abilities and practices. The short version of Deconfliction is this: "Give respect to get respect."

CHAPTER 4

THE 10 DECONFLICTION PRINCIPLES:

Situational Awareness

Use Your Words

Active Listening

Empathy

Find Common Ground

Acknowledge the Problem

Confront Negative Feelings

Encourage Compromise

Give Choices

Be Positive

SITUATIONAL AWARENESS:

The term situational awareness, which became trendy during the war against terrorism era, as a notion has been around since Sun Tzu wrote the original *The Art of War* (Tzu, 475 and 221 B.C.E.) and the term can also be traced to WWI (Gilson, 1995). Situational awareness serves as a baseline or foundation for future decisions and continues throughout a situation.

There is also a constant type of situational awareness, which is slightly different. Being aware of the surroundings is also being situationally aware, but it's related more to personal safety. What is addressed in Deconfliction relates to the ability to recognize a mental state and read the room.

The ability to recognize common human behaviors in particular circumstances juxtaposed against odd or suspicious actions can save lives. Sometimes, people become too caught up in the moment and forget to identify what is slightly off.

The elements of situational awareness are

1. Check your emotional state.

2. Assess the demeanor of the citizen.

3. Don't convey arrogance.

When officers are nervous, aggression can take over, and a citizen can be hurt. In my time on the street, I am sure I ran headlong into situations without considering my mental or emotional state in light of the incident, which blinded my situational awareness. Fortunately, I left law enforcement with only a few battle scars. However, when I was working the street, police officers were not ambushed on a frequent basis. In 2020, ambush style attacks on police increased 90 percent by some accounts (Cochran, 2021). Officers must focus on personal safety-related situational awareness and their own mental and emotional state as well as the mental state of citizens.

The police academy, in my experience, centered much of the practical training on officer presence from the aspect of gaining and maintaining control of a situation without truly trying to understand the point of view of the citizen. Additionally, the training did not address being authoritative without portraying arrogant authority, which can generate a rebellious response in today's not so civil society.

Situational awareness is an important part of officer safety and consists of internal and external mental, psychological, and physiological responses to the particular immediate environment.

Outward threat recognition is a skill which can be taught. Inward reflection of a mental state and how it manifests in unhelpful behavior toward others can be exposed through

CHAPTER 4

criticism; however, positive change can only occur through personal introspection and subsequent modification of unproductive conduct.

In my example, Ashley's mother continued to make disparaging comments loud enough for the neighborhood to hear as I contemplated my next move. Mom was not helping the situation, which forced me to recommend she step outside. My patience was running thin, and I had to check my own emotional state.

Back in the hallway outside Ashley's door, I assessed her demeanor as one of needing someone to actually listen to her. I had a few options. I could force the door open to resolve the issue. I could give Ashley orders to open the door in a commanding and stern voice. Those alternatives seemed to be more of the same of what Ashley was already receiving at home.

My officer presence became one of "I am on your side."

"Ashley, can you please open the door and tell me what's going on?" I heard the lock click. Ashley invited me into the room. I assessed all Ashley needed was someone who was open to listening to her, so I gave her the opportunity to tell her story.

USE YOUR WORDS:

Communication is key. Clear communication could be a matter of life and death. At the very least, the right words in the right tone and the right delivery can resolve a situation without incident.

The elements of using your words are

1. Choose your words carefully.

2. Don't be condescending.

3. Explain your actions.

"Use your words" is related to situational awareness, meaning you must keep your emotions in check.[14] "Don't make it personal" and "Think before you speak" are two timeless adages.

The "Practicals" at the police academy, as I remember, focused mostly on delivering commands to control the situation through loud and clear instructions, which in certain circumstances is necessary and others a detriment. If you allow your emotions to take over calm and rational thinking, then the words you speak may provoke a rebellious response. This can ultimately derail any efforts to control the situation.

Loud, clear, and simple instructions are useful when tensions are high, and everyone involved in the moment seems on edge. In this type of environment, calming the tone of the words spoken and using more encouraging phrases can keep the hostilities deconflicted. People respond to humanity. In the midst of a crisis situation, telling someone "Everything is all right" and "Let's just get through this" can cut through the perceived and real resentments.

Resist the urge to say "Calm down" or "Just relax" as these words can be construed as condescending or actual demands. Choosing your words can become even more important in seemingly innocuous situations like a young teenage girl locked in her bedroom.

---

[14] Experts say that all it takes is a raised middle finger to trigger the brain's "rage system," which shuts down rational decision-making and activates the "fight or flight" response, sending adrenaline pulsing through the bloodstream and preparing limbs for battle. When people experience normal anger, they feel frustrated but can still weigh pros and cons and solve problems. When they are enraged, they become irrational, lashing out at anyone around them, including those they love, said anger expert Ron Potter-Efron, who has authored half a dozen books on the subject, including one titled *Rage*. Many report feeling as though their bodies have been taken over. In extreme states, they may black out and forget what they did. "It overpowers the brain and literally shuts down the sensory systems and the power of reason," said W. Doyle Gentry, author of *Anger Management for Dummies* and founding editor of the *Journal of Behavioral Medicine*. "You are literally out of your mind," he said (Colvin, 2009).

CHAPTER 4

Don't preach or tell someone what to think or feel. Don't impose your morality. This may seem simple enough. However, people are more inclined to express their personal views, which on social media can be harmless at best, or mean and hateful at worst, but when engaged in a law enforcement action, this type of rhetoric can cause adverse reactions.

"Do what I tell you." These words, most likely, have been uttered by every law enforcement officer at some point in their career. Better words would be "I need you to (insert command here)." Follow up with something like "Please, I am just trying to keep everyone safe." Most citizens understand law enforcement officers are just doing their jobs and want to comply but also want to be treated with dignity.

Aside from using soothing words in a high stress situation, law enforcement officers must communicate effectively when questioning someone in various circumstances. One technique of effective interviewing is called parroting, which is taught in many interviewing courses, which is described as, "A conversational technique that can be quite effective in therapy. The therapist loosely repeats what the client has just said. The twin goals of this technique are ensuring that the therapist heard what was said correctly and encouraging the client to further clarify his or her thoughts" (Fritscher, 2021). However, Fritscher adds the caveat, "When parroting, it is important not to go too far. It is much better to repeat only the last few words than to attempt to repeat several sentences. Additionally, repetitive parroting can become annoying. It can also make the client feel nervous or edgy" (2021). Parroting can be interpreted as patronizing or not actually listening.

Words mean things. Communication in law enforcement is accomplished verbally the majority of time, and the remainder is done through body language. Therefore, choose your words carefully and be mindful of your body language, which can be perceived as a threat, disinterest, or a lack of respect.

I found through my experience that explaining why you are doing what you are doing goes a long way to disarming a citizen. The caution is to not engage in a debate on the street about constitutional rights or needing a warrant. As I told numerous trainees, ensure you are standing on firm legal ground for your actions, then be confident. This translates into telling a citizen the very basic legal reason for what you are doing. A simple explanation can go a long way to lower emotions without getting into an argument.

A law enforcement officer is accountable for what they say. It is almost better to say less than become provoked into saying something a citizen can include in a complaint. More importantly, not saying something provocative goes further to stabilizing a situation and leaving a more professional footprint.

Over my career in law enforcement, I began to notice more citizens who were unwilling to follow my simple commands. Citizens seemed to expect to be treated more humanely, rightly so, and voiced that expectation when I interacted with them. A dilemma arises when a law enforcement officer is trying to control the behavior of a citizen, who may be dangerous, as opposed to a citizen who is just upset about being stopped. There is a fine line between being polite and contemplating methods to subdue a hostile citizen.

Law enforcement officers must always consider what they are saying and how it is received or could be received when interacting with a citizen. A combination of explanation and commands could be more advantageous.

My calm voice, encouraging words, and truthful explanation to Ashley fostered the climate where she felt safe to open the door and have a conversation.

ACTIVE LISTENING:

Active listening is an important skill to learn, develop, practice, and utilize as a law enforcement officer. Actually, everyone would be better served with at least a little active listening (Lebow, 2021). Active listening requires the ability to concentrate on what someone is saying in order to respond and not just waiting on your turn to speak.

CHAPTER 4

The elements of active listening are

1. Listen carefully.

2. Let someone say their piece.

3. Use silence.

The physical act of hearing what someone is saying is important; however, it is only the initial step. If you hear what a person tells you but fail to comprehend what they are expressing, you will most likely not grasp their point of view.

Police officers are trained to intervene in situations and through experience tend to develop their own method of interacting with citizens. This typically manifests as providing advice, expressing thoughts, or giving directives. This process may interfere with citizens voicing their thoughts and concerns. Respect and trust become more resounding when citizens are offered the opportunity to say their piece. Everyone needs to be heard at times, which requires a law enforcement officer to suppress the urge to interrupt and allow the citizen to vent.

"The first one who speaks loses." This maxim is an interview technique often misunderstood and not followed by young energetic officers. The "awkward" silence is designed to spur spontaneous utterances by a suspect or any citizen for that matter. Ask a question, then stay silent. If the citizen starts talking, do not interrupt by asking another question. If someone wants to tell you something incriminating or important, do not get in their way. Remember, "during any moment of silence amid a suspect [or citizen] interview, the first side to break the silence typically loses the round" (Saladrigas, 2020). Better to remain silent or neutral and only acknowledge you heard what the person said.

During this time of silence and active listening, you can observe the body language of a citizen to determine if their affect is appropriate.[15] The caveat to this is people react differently to the same situation and body language is not always the best clue in determining the veracity of any statements.[16] If you find yourself saying, "They shouldn't have done that or acted that way," stop and instead scrutinize what they have said, and then continue to actively listen.

Ashley told me about her drawings and how her mother was always complaining about everything. I listened quietly, and she continued to talk about how she wanted to move out one day when she turned eighteen. I asked Ashley if she would speak to the paramedic about her mental state when I sensed the time was right, and she agreed without hesitation.

EMPATHY:

It can be said that empathy is the foundational principle which draws individuals into law enforcement. The typical answer to the question, "Why do you want to be a police officer?" is "I want to help people." This statement, by implication, indicates empathy. In law enforcement, empathy is an important character trait to have, and it can manifest in several ways. There is also a caveat to this attribute.

The elements of empathy are

1. Be aware of someone's feelings: positive and negative.

2. Alleviate distress; don't add to it.

3. Open up without being vulnerable.

---

[15] "Affect refers to the outward expression of a person's internal emotions. For most people, there is congruence between affect and circumstance..." (Cuncic, 2020).

[16] The book *Duped* by Timothy Levine discusses the truth default theory and, in his opinion, exposes body language reading to determine truthfulness as mere guesswork (Levine, 2020).

CHAPTER 4

Let's start off by reviewing a few definitions. Empathy is "the action of understanding, being aware of, being sensitive to, and vicariously experiencing the feelings, thoughts, and experience of another of either the past or present without having the feelings, thoughts, and experience fully communicated in an objectively explicit manner" (Merriam-Webster, n.d.).

Sympathy is closely related to empathy, but to fully understand empathy, it is constructive to review the difference between the two words.

Sympathy and empathy both refer to a caring response to the emotional state of another person, but a distinction between them is typically made; while sympathy is a feeling of sincere concern for someone who is experiencing something difficult or painful, empathy involves actively sharing in the emotional experience of the other person.

You can become more emotionally engaged in the plight of another human being when you empathize. This is when you truly feel their pain, discomfort, or concerns. You connect with the person, whereas sympathy tends to separate you from the other person (Psychiatric Medical Care Communications Team, 2022). As noted above, there is a caveat to this investment of emotion, which is discussed below.

These two qualities, empathy and sympathy, whether intrinsic or learned and practiced by law enforcement officials and citizens alike can create the conditions for a positive, successful police-citizen interaction.

Don't fake empathy or compassion. People are very perceptive, and they know when you are feigning emotions and concern. They will either call you out on it or refuse to deal with you. This is fundamental to human nature and interaction no matter if you are a law enforcement officer or a citizen.

The caveat about empathy is there must be a balance between opening up and becoming vulnerable. It is acceptable to share in the feelings of a citizen; however, keep your emotions in check, or you won't last. This holds true in any career constantly thrusting you into the most horrible states of the human condition. You will potentially be an emotional mess if you don't harden your heart. Allowing yourself to become emotionally vulnerable as a law enforcement officer can result in personal life attachment problems. Law enforcement officers can become detached from family members by not sharing their experiences. This may cause loved ones to feel isolated.

If you become detached from those close to you, the only catharsis you have from those dark moments is joking about the tragedies with other officers or alcohol. Stress experienced by officers can lead to risky behaviors like anonymous sex, impulse control leading to domestic violence, and other drugs. These behaviors are present within the law enforcement community across the United States.[17]

Law enforcement officers and citizens should strive to be a positive experience for each other. Empathy should be born out of mutual respect for the other human being irrespective of whether they are the police officer or citizen.

I gained Ashley's trust by showing empathy. She knew I was on her side, and I explained I had talked to many younger people who felt that their parents didn't listen to them as well.

FIND COMMON GROUND:

Finding common ground is a way to express empathy. Common ground "is a topic, opinion, or interest that two or more people can agree about" (Wooll, 2021). If it seems like you are at odds with the person, remember their true demeanor may be different than what you are seeing at that particular moment, and looking for common ground could pave the way to better understanding.

The elements of finding common ground are

---

[17] "Addiction within the law enforcement community across America is a widespread and serious problem. One out of four police officers on the street has an alcohol or drug abuse issue, and substance use disorders among police officers are estimated to range between 20% and 30% as compared to under 10% in the general population" (Cidambi, 2018).

CHAPTER 4

1. Build rapport.

2. Reassure them they are not alone.

3. Share a personal story.

Building rapport is a way to develop a positive relationship with another individual while fostering trust and respect (Brimbal & Hill, 2022). There are several ways to build rapport which mirror the elements of Deconfliction.[18] The desired outcome of building rapport is a better relationship between both the law enforcement official and the citizen which can lead to a positive outcome.

People find comfort in the fact they are not the only person who has ever experienced what they are going through (Johnson, 2019). You can share general details about others you have encountered with the same problems, but don't give too much detail as the citizen may believe you will talk about them to others later. The idiom "Misery loves company" can have a negative connotation; however, it can also suggest that people find solace in the fact they are not alone.

Sharing your own personal story to a citizen, as a police officer, carries the same caveat as showing empathy. Officers must always be vigilant when revealing personal information

---

[18] Rapport-building techniques in an information-gathering interview can include: Asking open-ended questions (e.g., "tell," "explain," "describe"), using affirmations (i.e., positive reinforcement, such as "Thank you, that was very helpful"), listening actively (e.g., use of encouragers, such as "go on, mm-hmm, etc.", repeating key words, echoing, evidence of turn-taking), summarizing a subject's account to demonstrate listening, using silence and avoiding interruptions to allow for subject disclosure, expressing empathy (people's ability to understand thoughts, feelings, and perspectives of another) without condoning illegal behavior, allowing a subject autonomy (i.e., providing room for the subject to talk in the conversation), showing interest in the subject as a person, displaying respect and patience, using evocation to draw out an individual's feelings and motives, and disclosing personal information and finding similarities with the subject (Brimbal & Hill, 2022)).

as the citizen or others who may be listening could use the knowledge against them. Provide enough information, when appropriate, to suggest common ground.

I didn't have my own story to reveal to Ashley; however, sharing my experiences with other teenagers having issues with their parents went a long way to building rapport with her.

ACKNOWLEDGE THE PROBLEM:

People like to be heard. When you acknowledge their problem, it's an indication they are the focus of your attention. This goes far to convey that you do care about what they have to say and what they are currently going through in their life.

The elements of acknowledging the problem are

1. Clarify the problem.

2. Restate the problem.

3. Address the problem directly.

Ask questions, if necessary, to ensure you are clear about the real problem. In the heat of the moment, people tend to verbalize many closely related issues, but it is best to discover the main problem or issue. People will correct you if they think you misunderstand.

Paraphrase the issue or problem once it has been clarified to reinforce that you understand. This will communicate your willingness to focus on their problem (Miller, 2008).

Don't avoid the elephant in the room. Once the issue or problem is clear, address it directly. If you are uncomfortable talking about the subject, get over it. Evading the problem is dismissive and can lead to further negativity. People will appreciate your taking the time to listen and recognize their troubles.

CHAPTER 4

Ashley responded in a positive way once I determined her problems stemmed from an overbearing mother, and I talked about those difficulties specifically.

CONFRONT NEGATIVE FEELINGS:

If negative feelings are not challenged, they can grow through tacit acceptance. Confronting those negative feelings should be approached in a tactful way to avoid reinforcing or adding to any current negative thoughts.

The elements of confronting negative feelings are

1. Be assertive, not aggressive.

2. Don't be accusatory or judgmental.

3. Understand why they are negative.

When confronting negative feelings or attitudes, it's best to be firm but not overly aggressive. A citizen who already has negative feelings about the police may expect the worst. If you, as a law enforcement officer, break the preconceived perception of police and show a human side, people tend to respond in a positive way.

Judgmental or accusatory language should not be uttered, even if you are attempting to have them admit to something. People do not want to be judged. If you judge someone because they are projecting negativity, they will believe you don't care and assume you are not listening to their concerns (Wright, 2022).

Asking questions may expose why the citizen has negative feelings, which could give some insight into why they have these feelings. When you understand where the person is coming from, you can then potentially direct the conversation to overcome those feelings.

Ashley seemed skeptical at first as I talked to her through the door. She may have assumed I was just another adult who was going to tell her what to do, not listen nor try to understand what she was feeling. It was rewarding to prove her wrong.

ENCOURAGE COMPROMISE:

Let the negotiations begin. Compromise is cooperation, and seeking it will give a citizen a stake in the outcome. Guide the person toward possible ways to resolve the issue.

The elements of encouraging compromise are

1. Collaborate.

2. Solicit a resolution.

3. Keep an open mind.

Working together with someone can turn their attention to thinking of ways to solve the problem at hand. This negation skill includes the person in the problem-solving process (Miller, 2008).

Once the person acquiesces to becoming a part of the solution, extract ideas from them to determine the best outcome. Solicit as many potential answers as possible in case one or several are unreasonable.

Keep an open mind and stay open to suggestions. A combination of solutions could produce the best possible outcome. Remember, there are definitely times to compromise, especially when you remain in the negotiation phase, and the situation has not escalated.

I asked Ashley how she hoped to resolve the overarching issues in the grand scheme of things after understanding why she was rebellious. She talked about her dream of being an artist, moving out, and going to college. It was good to hear she had a plan.

CHAPTER 4

GIVE CHOICES:

"Our parents bring us into the world, but in the end, we are responsible for what we become." - Kahlil Gibran

The choices we make shape our future. It is a luxury to have several choices. Choices can foster a sense of hope in people, which will go a long way in keeping the situation calm and under control.

The elements of giving choices are

1. Provide realistic choices.

2. Discuss the consequences of the choices.

3. Reach a resolution.

Present realistic choices that can actually be accomplished. If you present a choice which ultimately can't be delivered, you will lose respect. However, if a choice at first is ostensibly deliverable, but later becomes impossible, you must quickly and honestly explain the reasons why. People understand law enforcement officers are only doing their job, and most citizens can appreciate there are other forces which have a say in what occurs beyond the control of the officer.

Choices have consequences. You must discuss the consequences related to each choice presented in an open and honest way. It will be more productive if you can discuss the possible outcomes of the choices in a more positive way. People are more likely to respond in a sanguine way when they know what could happen to them, especially when it comes to their freedom and liberty.

A solution to the current situation and possible future situations should be the goal. Citizens expect law enforcement to solve their problems, especially when the police are answering a call for service. Officers are also expected to settle problems even when police contact citizens without prompting from the citizen. If the citizen is included in the resolution process, it has a greater potential of ending constructively.

Although I could not deliver on the choices Ashley presented to settle the problem, I explained to her, for now, she needed to go along with being evaluated by a crisis counselor and possibly go to the hospital for a psychiatric evaluation. I told her cooperating now would put her in a better position in a few years when she turned eighteen, and she could move out and follow her dreams. The consequences of resisting could have negative consequences for her later in life.

BE POSITIVE:

A positive attitude is key. "According to the positive mental attitude philosophy, a positive mindset is synonymous with hope, optimism, courage, and kindness. It also means not giving in to negativity and hopelessness even in difficult situations" (Perry, 2021). If you project a positive attitude, a condescending tone should not be detected.

The elements of being positive are

1. Avoid negativity.

2. Remain calm.

3. Always say thank you.

It can be difficult to avoid negativity, but it is important to recalibrate the negative aspects of a police citizen encounter into something positive. Law enforcement officers focus on the negative typically because they are problem solvers. This mindset does not support a constructive encounter with a citizen.

Remain calm! Easier written than done at times. Some officers take conflict to heart and make it personal. Officers with experience tend not to take confrontations with citizens personally because they have learned over the years that it is not always personal. They have also learned if they are calm and more relaxed, citizens will usually mirror their demeanor. It's better not to provoke an emotional reaction from a citizen.

Lastly, thank someone for their cooperation even if they were not exactly cooperating. This element of being positive, thanking someone, can be the last thing said, but it's not necessarily the only time to thank someone. Thanking someone is being polite and respectful, and if you are polite, chances are the citizen will thank you as well.

I remained calm and spoke in a gentle tone with Ashley throughout the entire incident. I can't say I did the same when speaking to her mother. In the end, Ashley happily agreed to speak to a counselor via video conference and was found not to be a danger to herself or anyone, even her mother. I thanked Ashley for being the adult in the house and gave her one last pep talk about acquiescing to her mother's wishes for a few more years. She agreed, which was all the thanks I needed.

FINAL THOUGHT:

Deconfliction is a mindset, as noted at the start of this chapter. All ten Deconfliction Principles are important and operate independently of each other. A situation can remain calm, professional, and controlled even if only a few of the principles of Deconfliction are utilized during a police-citizen contact. Moreover, remember it is a mindset, not a step-by-step set of instructions to a successful police-citizen contact.

Despite this chapter addressing the actions, attitudes, and thought process of law enforcement officers during interactions with citizens, Deconfliction should also be utilized by citizens. The Deconfliction mindset can bring civility back into everyday contact between everyone.

CHAPTER 5

DECONFLICTION IN ACTION

This chapter will recount a few stories to highlight the applied Deconfliction Principles. The stories are from my personal interactions with citizens as a law enforcement officer. Keep in mind, these situations came before the Deconfliction concept. Deconfliction was born out of a retrospective review of past situations.

It can be enlightening to scrutinize your experiences from an academic point of view. You can gain insight into your behaviors and reactions to incidents, and in doing so, you can grow emotionally and intellectually. Law enforcement officers should be performing an after-action review following every citizen contact.

I will post the elements of each Deconfliction concept at the beginning of the scenarios to allow the reader to practice analyzing how they were utilized. The more you learn to look for certain behaviors, the better you will be at recognizing them in your own police-citizen encounters.

SITUATIONAL AWARENESS:

The elements of situational awareness:
1. Check your emotional state.

2. Assess the demeanor of the citizen.

3. Don't convey arrogance.

Early in my career, I responded to a "46," code for "officer needs assistance." An officer ran into a nightclub alone after a 911 call was placed regarding a large melee inside the club. The officer was quickly shoved to the ground and kicked repeatedly.

The adrenaline pumped through my veins as I drove to the scene on a rain-soaked roadway. Maybe I was driving too fast for the conditions. As I approached an intersection, another officer, who was also responding to the scene, came from a side street and stopped for the red light but unfortunately stopped right in my path. I was able to go around him; however, the Ford Crown Victoria I was driving did not like the wet road, and I lost control. I slammed into a parked car, pushing it completely onto the sidewalk, and spun two complete revolutions, bouncing off of two more parked vehicles. My emotional situational awareness drowned in my heightened sense of excitement and desire to assist a fellow officer. Thankfully, I emerged from the vehicle, with the assistance of a homeless man who happened to be nearby, without any injuries. I did have the green light, but because I had not learned to control the adrenaline flowing through my veins in high stress situations, I was driving too fast. I trained myself over the years to calm my mind, control my breathing, and slow down my thinking to clearly understand what was occurring around me. It's like a Formula 1 racer who can navigate a twisting and turning track at speeds over 200 mph.

Situational awareness is a skill that can be valuable to anyone and can even be applied in everyday life. Think of a time where you would like to go back to and handle the situation differently and consider how it could have turned out if you practiced some situational awareness as described in the Deconfliction Principles.

Many years later in my career, I stopped a vehicle around 3:00 a.m. and had an uneasy feeling while talking to the driver. I noticed the vehicle after the driver went from a local hotel and briefly stopped at two different convenience stores without going inside. I initiated a traffic stop after the driver failed to use his turn signal. I asked the driver where he was headed, and he said he was going to a convenience store to get a drink. This was odd since I had just watched him stop at two stores minutes earlier. He was friendly but clearly nervous. I noticed a heavy jacket on the front passenger seat, and he had his hand on top of the coat as he spoke to me through the passenger window. My situational awareness was tingling, and I suspected he had something, possibly a gun, under the coat. I remained calm and asked for his license. I called for my partner to come and back me up; however, he was occupied and unable to respond. The traffic stop occurred on a highway with occasional traffic. The driver was a big guy, and I assessed if he did not cooperate, there would be a struggle. His license was valid, and my partner still was not able to back me up. I decided that without any further probable cause and no other officer able to assist, it was not worth asking him to exit the vehicle. Sometimes it is better to listen to your inner voice and avoid a potential confrontation.

USE YOUR WORDS:

The elements of using your words:

1. Choose your words carefully.

2. Don't be condescending.

3. Explain your actions.

DECONFLICTION: DON'T BE A STATISTIC

Jason and I received several calls to assist a mother with her twenty-something-year-old son who had anger issues along with other mental illnesses. He was tall and appeared to be extraordinarily strong, and he was prone to fits of rage that manifested in breaking items in his house. The mother tried to get him help, but he refused. The son was pacing outside under the car port when Jason and I arrived. Jason had built a rapport with the kid from previous calls, so it was best for Jason to approach first. Jason talked to the kid in a friendly tone to let him know we were there to help. The kid always complained about his mother and how she supposedly treated him. Jason explained to him we were only there to make sure everyone was safe. I spoke to the mother as Jason kept the son calm. I listened to the mother complain about needing her son out of the house because she was just not able to deal with him. I told the mother she should go to family court and attempt to prove to the judge her son needed psychiatric care to get him the help he needed, but we could not force him to go to the hospital since he did not appear to be a threat to himself or others. The situation was always delicate because we did not want to upset her son, which could cause him to have an anger outburst. Law enforcement officers tend to give lectures, which at times is exactly the wrong approach. Lectures can be perceived as talking down to someone, causing them to become defensive. Many people have a professional voice that is very cold, direct, and robotic. When you hear it, you recognize it, and it may leave you wondering if the person is truly human. It can be more inviting to choose words which seem less rehearsed and more like a friendly conversation.

Sometimes, too much talk is just too much. At one point, Jason and I both had trainees, one younger and one older. The younger wanted to save the world, and the older was just trying to pass field training. One slow shift after midnight, we received a call about a strange man knocking on someone's door asking for money. When we arrived on scene, the trainees contacted a homeless man who was intoxicated. Jason and I stood back and allowed the trainees to handle the situation. They were very

CHAPTER 5

polite and asked the man many questions to determine what he was doing, and his answer was he was trying to get money. The trainees wanted to take the man to the homeless shelter, but the shelter closed at 8 p.m., and the shelter would not take people who were intoxicated.

Jason and I talked while the trainees tried to determine how they could help this man who was knocking on strangers' doors at 1:00 a.m. After almost an hour, Jason and I had enough. We stepped in and told the man to disperse from the area and stop knocking on doors, or we would take him to jail for public intoxication. Minutes later, we cleared the call. Sometimes, the direct approach is the best.

ACTIVE LISTENING:

The elements of active listening:

1. Listen carefully.

2. Let someone say their piece.

3. Use silence.

I was handed an open-and-shut theft case as a detective. An iPad, which was part of an embezzlement case, was stolen from the office of a former employee of the Charleston County Consolidated Dispatch Center. When the iPad was discovered as missing, detectives reviewed the video and observed a security guard going into the office during his overnight shift and, a few minutes later, leaving the office with something visible inside his shirt. I asked the guard to come in and speak with me as we needed to recover the iPad. It was always curious to me when I invited someone to come to the Sheriff's Office to talk, and they never asked why. I printed a few photos from the video showing a rectangular object inside the guard's shirt and had them at the ready during the interview.

DECONFLICTION: DON'T BE A STATISTIC

I started the interview by asking the guard about his daily routine, explaining how some issues had arisen at the dispatch center. I actively listened, showing great interest in his daily routine. The guard still had not asked why he was asked to come in and speak to a detective. I finally directed him to where I wanted the conversation to go and asked him about entering offices. The video showed the guard entering the office where the iPad was located and exiting just over two minutes later. The guard told me he never went into locked offices unless maybe he thought he smelled smoke or thought there was a problem, but he would only open the door and look in without really going inside. The trap was set.

I told the guard an iPad had been taken from one of the offices, and I was tasked with investigating who may have stolen it. The guard sucked the air out of the room. I asked him for his opinion on how someone could have removed an iPad without being caught on video. He offered several theories such as placing the iPad in a backpack or lunch bag. The one theory he never did float was someone hiding the iPad under their shirt even though I pressed him for more ideas.

I then asked the guard straight out if he took the iPad, to which he responded with a resounding no, and he added he never went into the office in question.

The trap was sprung.

I pulled out the photos from a folder, and the first one I revealed was the guard going into the office. The second pic was of him coming out of the office, and the third photo showed the iPad inside his shirt. He immediately had an excuse. The guard told me the shape under his shirt was his bullet proof vest curling up at the bottom. It was clearly not his vest. I asked the guard if he would take a polygraph, and he agreed. I said I had to check with the polygrapher to determine if he was available, which I actually did prior to the interview.

A few minutes later, I went back into the interview room and sat quietly for a moment. I leaned in and, in a low, calm voice, offered some redemption. I told him we all make mistakes, and it is always better to own up to them. I sat back and waited.

CHAPTER 5

The silence was deafening. The guard eventually looked up and, in a soft voice, admitted to taking the iPad. He explained how it was his wife's fault for taking the iPad. His granddaughter broke the one they owned, and he didn't want to hear his wife complain about it, so his plan was to borrow the one he took until the other could be fixed. Later in the day, the guard turned over the stolen iPad.

EMPATHY:

The elements of empathy:

1. Be aware of someone's feelings: positive and negative.

2. Alleviate distress; don't add to it.

3. Open up without being vulnerable.

I have been to some horrific scenes throughout my career. Homicides and car accidents can be the most shocking. I can picture some of those events like they happened yesterday, and not to sound melodramatic, those experiences changed me.

I will always remember many of my experiences; however, one event probably affected me the most. Early in my career, it was the day before graduation at the College of Charleston, and a group of four students were happily driving along the streets of downtown Charleston. The front passenger was a young, blonde girl, who just finished her undergraduate degree and was ready to celebrate and move forward with the rest of her life. It was night shift when I came upon an accident. A dark sedan was on its roof along the right-hand curb. I approached the vehicle, and the blonde girl was lying face up with her legs in the air, half in and half out of the vehicle. I reached down, shook her, asked if she was all right, and checked for a pulse. I could feel her heart beating. The fire department arrived and took over the scene. As I stepped back, a bystander pointed to a young man standing in the middle of the street and said he was driving a van, ran the red light, and struck the sedan. I grabbed his arm and placed him in the back of my police cruiser. I turned around to see the firefighters placing a tarp around the girl; it was then I knew she was no longer among the living.

Feeling the last heartbeats of a college student is tough to process. Sometimes heartbreaking events in your personal life intersect with situations in your law enforcement career. My mother passed away in 2014. In 2016, I was working Christmas Eve when I was dispatched to the scene of a car accident. When I arrived, I was told a woman ran off the road and struck a tree, killing her instantly. The fire department was working to extricate her from the mangled wreck. I was researching where she lived and possible relatives. The coroner arrived and pronounced the death. I provided the coroner with the woman's address, which was only a few miles from the accident. There was no answer at the residence. Dispatch was able to locate a phone number for a possible relative. I called and contacted the former father-in-law of the woman. It was about 3 a.m. when we finally reached the former in-laws and broke the news of the death of their daughter-in-law. They were visibly upset, but they were also worried about how the grandkids would take the news. It was now Christmas morning.

The woman had two kids, a daughter who was about 25 and a son about 27-years-old. The former in-laws, the coroner, and I all traveled to the daughter's apartment and arrived around 5 a.m. The brother lived close by and was called to come over.

The living room was filled with Christmas cheer and a beautiful tree with presents stacked underneath. The news the coroner conveyed broke the spirit of all who could hear. Empathy, real and personal, hung in the air that Christmas morning.

FIND COMMON GROUND:

The elements of finding common ground:

CHAPTER 5

1. Build rapport.

2. Reassure them they are not alone.

3. Share a personal story.

There are varying degrees of mental illness, and often, people who are suffering from a mental illness are not being treated. This is a growing dilemma officers face every day, and the scene control techniques taught at the academies can actually aggravate the situation (More in Chapter 7).

When called to the scene of an individual diagnosed with schizoaffective disorder, a law enforcement officer can prepare for the encounter. We had a reoccurring call to a residence where the 20-year-old daughter had bipolar disorder and could be violent or nonresponsive.

The family went to court and asked the judge to rule on their motion and order the daughter be taken to a facility for mental health treatment. The order was granted, and the sheriff's office had the duty to take her to a treatment facility. I responded to assist in the hopes the girl would comply without a struggle.

Upon arrival, I learned she had gone to her bedroom and locked the door. I tapped on the window and asked her to talk to me. She opened the window, and we had a nice conversation where I asked her how she was doing all the while I could hear her father ranting inside the house. I explained I was there only to help her, and she was not alone even though her family seemed apathetic and weary of her condition. I asked her if she could help me out by doing me the favor of coming outside. She shut the window and appeared at the front door. The transporting deputy arrived soon, and she went willingly for treatment.

CONFRONT NEGATIVE FEELINGS:

The elements of confronting negative feelings:

DECONFLICTION: DON'T BE A STATISTIC

1. Be assertive, not aggressive.

2. Don't be accusatory or judgmental.

3. Understand why they are negative.

Sometimes, a mother's love and protection of her daughter go off the rails. The mother of a 5-year-old girl filed a police report alleging her daughter was being abused by her kindergarten teachers. The accusation levied was how the teachers were not allowing the kindergartner to eat lunch, along with locking her in the closet and banishing the girl to the hallway.

The fact the complaint rose to the level of a police report on its face didn't seem right. The first few thoughts I had were: did the mother address this with the teachers or the school administration, was the mother receiving accurate information, and finally how stable was the mother.

I started my investigation with the school principal to determine if the mother made the same complaint to the school and if there were other complaints about the teacher and her assistant. There were no other complaints, and the mother did ask to speak with the principal, but the mother said she was too busy to talk every time she was approached. Video of the hallway showed no indication of the kindergartner being left in the hallway alone.

I interviewed the teacher and assistant separately, and they both conveyed similar information. The assistant broke down in tears at the thought of being accused of mistreating a student. They explained the young girl did not like to eat her lunch, and often, they let the girl keep her food well after the lunch hour, but eventually they had to take the lunch away. I was also told the mother sent her daughter to school with an adult *Ensure* protein drink because she was underweight for her age. As for being locked in a closet, it was part of an active shooter drill the entire school conducted, and all of the kids were hustled into a large storage room within the classroom.

CHAPTER 5

I called the mother several times to explain my findings and was only able to leave several voicemails for her to call me back. She never called until I sent her a letter telling her I was closing the case as unfounded.

The call came one afternoon. The mother was irate on the phone, accusing me of being evil, not human, and basically an idiot. I told the mother I was sorry she felt like she did; however, there was just no merit to the accusations she made against the teachers, and I conveyed everything I had uncovered about the situation. The mother, in the end, wished me great harm and indicated she was going to call and report me to the FBI for not protecting her rights. I urged her to call the FBI and take any steps she felt necessary. She hung up on me.

ACKNOWLEDGE THE PROBLEM:

The elements of acknowledging the problem:

1. Clarify the problem.

2. Restate the problem.

3. Address the problem directly.

Some calls for service make you just shake your head and laugh. However, making fun of someone or humiliating them should never be tolerated as it is not only unprofessional but also rude.

Tammi was a "frequent flyer" for calling medical personnel (EMS) and the police for various issues. As the story goes, Tammi was some sort of New York model in her heyday, which was in the 1970s, and she apparently indulged in the party life.

One late afternoon, the call went out where Tammi needed assistance. I arrived before EMS knocked on the door and announced myself. Tammi answered the door not wearing a stitch of clothing. I was thankful the storm door separated us. I turned away and asked her to put on some clothes. Tammi was clearly intoxicated with a drink in hand. She disappeared from view and returned minutes later wearing a T-shirt and shorts.

Tammi said something about needing her medication and wanting to go to the hospital. I asked if she needed to talk to someone and if she was thinking of hurting herself. Her only response was something about how handsome I was, which she said to all officers and firefighters. I told Tammi we would get her some help as EMS and firefighters arrived. I quickly left her in capable hands.

Another woman who called the police often had a vastly different issue. The elderly woman lived alone except for the CIA spy living in her attic. Apparently, due to her late husband's dealings with the government, the CIA stationed a man in her attic to listen to her conversations and keep an eye on her. She pointed to a lawn mower in her yard which was mysteriously repaired as evidence of people watching her. My initial thought was that the noises she heard coming from the attic were from squirrels hiding their nuts. The best way to manage this type of situation is to acknowledge what the person hears or maybe sees is real to them without saying you hear or see the same thing. Ensure the person you will be there if they have any further concerns. Many times, people like this are just lonely and need someone to talk with.

ENCOURAGE COMPROMISE:

The elements of encouraging compromise:

1. Collaborate.

2. Solicit a resolution.

3. Keep an open mind.

CHAPTER 5

Domestic violence calls are some of the most dangerous calls for law enforcement. Officers can be ambushed by the primary aggressor of the violence for fear of going to jail. This example is not one of those.

Domestic arguments between particular couples, in my experience, seemed to occur in clusters. One such couple had disputes over trivial situations such as who misplaced the television remote control. On different occasions, the male half just wanted to sleep, but the female kept waking him up. This was clearly an epic dispute. I asked them both how we could resolve this issue. She suggested he leave and go to a friend's house. He wanted to stay as it was late, and he didn't want to wake anyone up. Middle East peace talks were easier. To resolve their problems, this couple needed to work it out between each other. I suggested an accord between the two where she stayed in her room, and he went to a different part of the house to sleep. Crisis averted.

GIVE CHOICES:

The elements of giving choices:

1. Provide realistic choices.

2. Discuss the consequences of the choices.

3. Reach a resolution.

Certain calls for service trigger an emotional response in some law enforcement officers. A vulnerable adult not being treated with respect, empathy, and consideration was a situation that could set my hair on fire.

The day before Thanksgiving, I was dispatched to an apartment complex regarding an eviction. I spoke to the property owner who showed me eviction paperwork for an older woman who failed to pay her rent. The property manager told me the woman had mental issues.

I went to speak with the woman and learned she was a former dispatcher who had a mental breakdown. I asked her if she had any place to stay, any family or friends who could take her in temporarily. She had no one. She told me she would have to sleep in her car. This was unacceptable. I contacted crisis intervention to see if they could find her a place for the night as it was approaching 7:00 p.m., and the temperature was dropping. A crisis team responded but determined there was nothing they could do for the woman. She was not a danger to herself or others, so they could not involuntarily commit her.

I approached the property owner and manager and explained the situation. I suggested they allow the woman to stay one more night until we could find a place for her. The property owner refused and wanted the woman out. My response was to refuse to evict the woman. I told the property manager I would not put an older woman out on the street to sleep in her car the night before Thanksgiving, and since they had been trying to get this woman out for months, one more night would not matter.

The property manager reluctantly agreed, and the crisis team indicated they would work on finding the woman a place to go the following morning. [19]

BE POSITIVE:

The elements of being positive:

---

[19] The property manager went to the judge who signed the eviction notice the following day, and the judge ordered me to stand before her. Charleston County Magistrate Judge Ellen Steinberg admonished me for not following her court order. She followed up with how she knew and respected how compassionate I was and the difficult position I faced, but next time, she expected I enforce her court orders. I respected Judge Steinberg, and we had some good conversations after court, and I think I can honestly say I believe she agreed with how I handled the situation but could not express her true thoughts in court, on the record, in front of the property owner.

CHAPTER 5

1. Avoid negativity.

2. Remain calm.

3. Always say thank you.

A trainee and I responded to an alarm call at a residence where the alarm company could not reach the homeowner. When we arrived there, a man in the driveway was loading items into a SUV, which was backed in. We approached the man and asked for identification. He immediately became enraged and stated he lived at the residence. I calmly explained to him we were dispatched to a burglar alarm, and we needed to verify he in fact lived at the residence. He continued yelling and accusing us of profiling him because he was black. We told the man it was standard procedure to determine the identity of a resident, and in this case since he was loading things into a vehicle, it was imperative we make sure he belonged there.

As the man continued to yell, an older gentleman appeared from the backyard and identified himself as the homeowner and the father of the man we were speaking with. The older man said his son suffered from mental illness.

We maintained our composure, expressed why we were there in a clear manner, and we were firm but polite. We thanked both parties for their cooperation, even though it was not immediate. Sometimes all you can do is explain the job you have to do and why you are doing what you are doing, and trust people will accept and respect the information.

The examples above of the Deconfliction Principles in action demonstrate their utility. Remember, the Deconfliction Principles are a mindset, whereas de-escalation is reactionary. The Deconfliction Principles are proactive and are meant to influence how police and citizens interact in a positive manner from the start of the encounter.

CHAPTER 6

SYSTEMIC RACISM IN LAW ENFORCEMENT

Systemic racism in law enforcement is a topic fraught with nuances, skewed data, emotions, political pitfalls, subjective self-serving statements, and outright lies.

This chapter is not an attempt to convince, persuade or build consensus regarding systemic racism within the criminal justice system. The goal is to potentially reduce the number of violent encounters between law enforcement and citizens, especially minority citizens, by moving the conversation closer to some sort of understanding about race relations and how those feelings and behaviors towards each other plays a role in those encounters. [20] Knowing the sensitivities of others, police officers and citizens alike can integrate the Deconfliction Principles into an interaction to hopefully arrive at a positive resolution.

---

[20] "One of the main barriers to the discussion and resolution of the issue of racism in the criminal justice system involves the multiple uses and meanings of the term racism. Definitions of this term range from a conscious attitude by an individual to an unconscious act by an institution or even to the domination of society by white culture. I have suggested that the term racism be abandoned in favor of the term racial prejudice (an attitude) and racial discrimination (an act)" (Wilbanks, 1987).

DECONFLICTION: DON'T BE A STATISTIC

I look forward to discussing how the Deconfliction Principles are incorporated with better race relations in other forums. (To discuss this and other related topics join me on Instagram or X at MrDeconfliction.) Until then, ponder the utility of each Deconfliction Principle for this specific topic.

A caveat: This chapter was written incorporating my own personal experiences and biases. Full disclosure, from my own experiences and perspective I don't believe the criminal justice system as constructed is systemically racist. I think that the criminal justice system, as it is now, is not systemically racist. In the past, for sure. But I think now the criminal justice system goes to great lengths to identify and root out those who are prejudiced. For clarity, I am only including law enforcement agencies, courts, and the legislature who pass criminal statutes within the criminal justice system. In the scope of the criminal justice system, I do not include other socioeconomic reasons that may account for criminal behavior or the disproportionate incarceration rate of minorities. The economic reasons tend to be conflated with systemic racism in law enforcement, which is not necessarily comparing similar concepts.

However, I will acknowledge I have absolutely witnessed individuals within law enforcement act upon racial bias. Additionally, I as a white male could never truly understand how a minority feels when encountered by a police officer. I hope over my law enforcement career I presented a fair and uniform treatment of everyone I encountered despite their race, religion or ethnicity.

I encourage you to review many different studies related to systemic racism in law enforcement and scrutinize the language. Focus on the word choice including ideas left wanting of an explanation. Do this for both sides of the systemic racism in law enforcement argument.

All the above being written, let's review some theories refuting the notion that the criminal justice system is systemically racist and others that reinforce the assertion regarding systemic racism within the criminal justice system.

CHAPTER 6

In 1986, Dr. William Wilbanks, a criminal justice professor with the Florida International University published the book, *The Myth of a Racist Criminal Justice System*, wherein he theorized it was a myth that the criminal justice system was racist. A subsequent article related to the book was published in 1987 stating, "at every point from arrest to parole, there is little or no evidence of an overall racial effect, in that the percentage outcomes for Black people and white people are not hugely different. There is evidence, however, that some individual decision makers (e.g., police officers, judges) are more likely to give breaks to whites than to Black people. However, there appears to be an equal tendency for other individual decision makers to favor Black people over whites. This 'canceling-out' effect results in studies that find no overall racial effect" (Wilbanks, 1987). Would more detailed studies that are conducted objectively as possible assist this narrative?

More recent studies have focused on statistical analysis of racial bias in policing based on arrests and police shootings of racial minorities. The *Proceedings of the National Academy of Sciences* published articles in 2019 weakening the assertion regarding systemic police bias (MacDonald, 2020). Do more recent studies fully explore the reasonable suspicion, probable cause, and motivations behind arrests and shootings? Perhaps it's time for such a study.

In the other corner, proponents of the notion that systemic racism in the criminal justice system continue to assert several theories supporting that belief. Multiple books have been written on the topic, and I recommend reading different works if it's of interest. I will not be able to present every nuance, theory, study or explanation substantiating the proclamation regarding systemic racism remaining with the criminal justice system. However, here are a few to consider.

Some scholars argue that systemic racism in the criminal justice system is historic. One such argument says, "Systemic and structural racism are forms of racism that are pervasively and deeply embedded in and throughout systems, laws, written or unwritten policies, entrenched practices, and established beliefs and attitudes that produce, condone, and perpetuate widespread unfair treatment of people of color" (Braveman et al., 2022, as cited in Bonilla-Silva, 1997). If this is true, have we as a society made any progress over the last 100, 75 or 50 years?

Researchers at the prestigious Harvard and other institutes propose that diverting funds away from the police and to the community will subsequently diminish the need for police in certain communities. "Diverting resources from the police to better support community services including health care, housing, and education, and stronger economic and job opportunities. They argue that broader support for such measures will decrease the need for policing, and in turn reduce violent confrontations, particularly in over-policed, economically disadvantaged communities, and communities of color" (Walsh, 2021). Does this redirection of funds from the police to the community actually resolve the purported problem of systemic racism within the criminal justice system?

Individuals involved in the conversation regarding systemic racism in the criminal justice system use various definitions, concepts, and perspectives to explain the inequities, perceived or real, related to enforcing criminal laws.

Below are some of the various concepts and definitions related to racism and systemic racism. As you read them, ask yourself if they are helpful in moving the conversation forward in a productive manner. Could there be a better alternative to address the systemic racism issue?

RACISM

The concept of racism is widely thought of as simply personal prejudice, but in fact, it is a complex system of racial hierarchies and inequities. The micro level of racism, or individual level, are internalized and interpersonal racism. The macro level of racism looks beyond the individuals to the broader dynamics, including institutional and structural racism ("Definition of Key Concepts and Constructs," 2022).

CHAPTER 6

INTERNALIZED RACISM

Internalized racism describes the private racial beliefs held by and within individuals. The way people absorb social messages about race and adopt them as personal beliefs, biases, and prejudices are all within the realm of internalized racism ("Definition of Key Concepts and Constructs," 2022).

For people of color, internalized oppression can involve believing in negative messages about oneself or one's racial group. For white people, internalized privilege can involve feeling a sense of superiority and entitlement or holding negative beliefs about people of color.

EXPLICIT VS. IMPLICIT BIAS

Explicit bias is the traditional conceptualization of bias. With explicit bias, individuals are aware of their prejudices and attitudes toward certain groups. Positive or negative preferences for a particular group are conscious. Overt racism and racist comments are examples of explicit biases.

Implicit bias involves all of the subconscious feelings, perceptions, attitudes, and stereotypes that have developed as a result of prior influences and imprints. It is an automatic positive or negative preference for a group, based on one's subconscious thoughts. However, implicit bias does not require animus; it only requires knowledge of a stereotype to produce discriminatory actions (U.S Department of Justice, n.d.).

INTERPERSONAL RACISM

Interpersonal racism is how our private beliefs about race become public when we interact with others. When we act upon our prejudices or unconscious bias—whether intentionally, visibly, verbally, or not—we engage in interpersonal racism. Interpersonal racism also can be willful and overt, taking the form of bigotry, hate speech, or racial violence ("Definition of Key Concepts and Constructs," 2022).

INSTITUTIONAL RACISM

Institutional racism is racial inequity within institutions and systems of power, such as places of employment, government agencies, and social services. It can take the form of unfair policies and practices, discriminatory treatment, and inequitable opportunities and outcomes ("Definition of Key Concepts and Constructs," 2022).

A school system that concentrates people of color in the most overcrowded and under-resourced schools with the least qualified teachers compared to the educational opportunities of white students is an example of institutional racism.

STRUCTURAL RACISM

Structural racism (or structural racialization) is the racial bias across institutions and society. It describes the cumulative and compounding effects of an array of factors that systematically privilege white people and disadvantage people of color ("Definition of Key Concepts and Constructs," 2022).

Since the word "racism" often is understood as a conscious belief, "racialization" may be a better way to describe a process that does not require intentionality. Race equity expert John A. Powell writes:

"'Racialization' connotes a process rather than a static event. It underscores the fluid and dynamic nature of race... 'Structural racialization' is a set of processes that may generate disparities or depress life outcomes without any racist actors" ("Definition of Key Concepts and Constructs," 2022).

CHAPTER 6

SYSTEMIC RACIALIZATION

Systemic racialization describes a dynamic system that produces and replicates racial ideologies, identities, and inequities. Systemic racialization is the well-institutionalized pattern of discrimination that cuts across major political, economic, and social organizations in a society ("Definition of Key Concepts and Constructs," 2022).

Public attention to racism is generally focused on the symptoms (such as a racist slur or the adultification of Black women and girls by an individual or group) rather than the system of racial inequity ("Definition of Key Concepts and Constructs," 2022).

RACIAL PRIVILEGE AND RACIAL OPPRESSION

Like two sides of the same coin, racial privilege describes race-based advantages and preferential treatment based on skin color while racial oppression refers to race-based disadvantages, discrimination, and exploitation based on skin color (Equity vs. Equality and Other Racial Justice Definitions, 2021).

SYSTEMIC RACISM

Policies and practices that exist throughout a whole society or organization, and that result in and support a continued unfair advantage to some people and unfair or harmful treatment of others based on race (Cambridge Dictionary, 2023).

SYSTEMIC RACISM AND AMERICA TODAY (BROOKINGS INSTITUTE):

"[T]he most hateful remnants of slavery persist in the U.S. today in the form of systemic racism baked into nearly every aspect of our society and who we are as a people. Indeed, for those tracing their heritage to countries outside of Western Europe, or for those with a non-Christian belief system, that undeniable truth often impacts every aspect of who you are as a person, in one form or another" (Allen, 2020).

Clearly, there are many definitions and concepts related to racism and racism within institutions. Do these aid in explaining the perceived racial issues within law enforcement or the criminal justice system? Perhaps they provide an explanation of racial disparities in rates of arrests, convictions, and incarcerations, and only obfuscate the failings of society, the breakdown of the family and morals, and the need of power brokers to point to a hidden enemy to perpetuate their positions. Could it be people act and react to their environment and not necessarily merely because of some latent historical racial bias?

Another method of understanding the state of systematic racism in law enforcement is to conduct a historical review of the path we as a country have taken. Jean de La Fontaine said, "A person often meets his destiny on the road he took to avoid it" (1819).

The 13th Amendment to the constitution was passed by the Senate in April of 1864 and then by the House of Representatives in January of 1865 (The Editors of Encyclopedia Britannica, 2016). The intent of the 13th Amendment was to abolish the tacit acquiescence of slavery within the constitution.

The passage of the 13th Amendment gave rise to "Jim Crow laws" in southern states. The Jim Crow laws[21] were "laws that

---

[21] Jim Crow was the name of a minstrel routine (actually Jump Jim Crow) performed beginning in 1828 by its author, Thomas Dartmouth ("Daddy") Rice, and by many imitators, including actor Joseph Jefferson. The term came to be a derogatory epithet for African Americans and a designation for their segregated life (Urofsky, 2023).

CHAPTER 6

enforced racial segregation in the South between the end of Reconstruction in 1877 and the beginning of the civil rights movement in the 1950s" (Urofsky, 2025). These laws perpetuated the control white Americans exerted over Black Americans, which infected law enforcement agencies throughout the country.

Jim Crow laws led to the Supreme Court being forced to address the elephant in the room. "In 1954, the Supreme Court reversed Plessy in Brown v. Board of Education of Topeka. It declared segregation in public schools unconstitutional, and by extension, the ruling was applied to other public facilities. In the years following, subsequent decisions struck down similar kinds of Jim Crow legislation" (Urofsky, 2025). However, even though the Supreme Court was finding laws steeped in racism unconstitutional, law enforcement maintained racist practices and turned a blind eye to racist behavior.[22]

Finally, the end to racist practices in the country to include within law enforcement systems came in 1964 in the form of the Civil Rights Act. At least that was the vision. The Civil Rights legislation was designed to "prohibited discrimination in public places, provided for the integration of schools and other public facilities, and made employment discrimination illegal. It was the most sweeping civil rights legislation since Reconstruction"" (National Archives, 2022).

Unfortunately, the Civil Rights Act did little to change the practices of some law enforcement agencies.

In reality, oversight of law enforcement by civilians started in the 1880s and until the 1920s police commissions were designed "to break the hold of political machines on local policing" (De Angelis et al., 2016). The commissioners were political appointees with little or no police experience who deferred to police commanders, which rendered the supervision ineffective.

From the 1920s to the 1960s, modern-day civilian review boards took shape, and although they were not adequately funded, they examined complaints against police and

---

[22] There are many examples of racist police departments and horrific police behavior. See, "Detroit Under Fire: Police Violence, Crime Politics, and the Struggle for Racial Justice in the Civil Rights Era" (Lassiter, 2020).

misconduct investigations internal to police agencies. These boards received opposition from police unions and local politicians, and in the end, they failed (De Angelis et al., 2016).

In the 70s and 80s, investigative bodies emerged from the Civil Rights Movement through protests of how police were treating African Americans. These boards had full investigative oversight with enhanced authority and resources (De Angelis et al., 2016).

Finally, in the 90s to present day, a hybrid form of civilian oversight models developed. These various investigative agencies began after the 1991 beating of Rodney King by police in Los Angeles. These agencies followed one of three models focusing on investigation, review, or auditing/monitor models.

The supervisory types of civilian review boards and internal police agency investigative divisions conduct investigations reactively, which are like most police investigations. Since it's not possible (yet) to read people's minds, a more productive approach might be to proactively review police citizen interactions based on contact cards, traffic tickets, and arrests.[23] The data collected on those cards could reveal a trend and potential racial biases of a particular officer.

An additional preemptive discovery of racial biases could call on fellow officers to report suspected racially motivated behavior to designated individuals within an agency. Yes, this sounds like an impossible idea considering the Thin Blue Line, but this must change to protect the integrity of policing.

I will share one of my experiences. A deputy I worked with, let's call him Aaron, was known for being aggressive and making many traffic stops often ending in finding guns, drugs, and many times both. It was also common knowledge he mainly stopped Black people. He seemed to have a bad case of tunnel

---

[23] Many police agencies require law enforcement officers to complete a citizen contact card or an FI (Field Interview) card whenever they interact with a citizen. Race and gender are items on those cards. Those cards are then turned in to a supervisor at the end of a shift. In South Carolina, in 2005, the legislature passed a law requiring law enforcement agencies to collect data related to age, race, and gender.

CHAPTER 6

vision during these traffic stops. On several occasions, he missed indicators that could have been deadly for him. Additionally, the probable cause he articulated was suspicious at best. I was working a night shift when I heard him call out a traffic stop which seemed odd. He said over the radio he was stopping a car because he observed it entering and exiting two different gas stations in a quick manner. Those gas stations were located so far apart it was next to impossible for Aaron to have followed the vehicle to each and then make the traffic stop in that amount of time. Also, there was no reason for him to provide the information about the two gas stations over the radio other than an attempt to establish probable cause. The driver was Black . In the end, Aaron didn't find any criminal activity afoot.

I routinely talked with supervisors regarding the less than professional and constitutional practices of Aaron. Those talks went nowhere. I don't fault the supervisors as they knew the complaints would be ignored at the high command level due to the police cultural practice of, if someone is making arrests, just ignore the rest. Typically, these types of actions are not fully investigated until something goes horribly wrong.

The caution to determining racial bias motivations in anyone, law enforcement officers or citizens, is that it's not necessarily easy to prove someone is acting because of racial animus. The media is quick to label an incident as racially motivated without anything more than a difference in the race of the parties involved. The cry of racism is almost always sounded when the law enforcement officer is white and the citizen is Black. Real proof a white officer was acting out of racial bias would only come after the incident was investigated.

The appearance of racism could be based upon the demographics of an area. If a specific city or neighborhood is comprised mostly of one race of people, it is logical that statistically more of that particular race would be arrested.[24] If statistics indicate police are killing more minorities per capita, does this automatically link racism or systemic racism to those incidents? A more comprehensive look at the total police-citizen interactions of a particular officer involved in a shooting could provide a clearer picture of whether the situation contained a racial component. Data manipulation, distorted reviews, and subjective interpretations do occur. It is naïve to think it does not happen.

Invoking racism as the main motivating factor for some police misconduct is lazy, disingenuous at least, and race-baiting at worst. Let's look at an incident in Memphis on January 7, 2023, to illustrate this point.

Tyre Nichols was pulled over by a street crimes unit in Memphis.[25] The five officers involved in beating Tyre to death during a traffic stop were Black . The media immediately pointed to systemic racism as the leading contributing factor. Additionally, "President Joe Biden adopted the racism narrative before much was known about the Nichols beating. Even before the videos from the officers' body cameras had been released, Biden was blaming Nichols's death on systemic racism. After the video release, Biden claimed the killing was representative of what Black and brown Americans experience every single day" (MacDonald, 2023). Moreover, "other Democrats spread that same message, amplified by the mainstream media. According to Rep. Jamaal Bowman (D-NY), Nichols was killed by 'white supremacy. Killed by America.' Blacks 'live in a constant

---

[24] The concept of community policing could be construed as racist; however, again it's not the practice itself it is how it's practiced. Racial profiling is a distinct possibility while conducting community policing. Racial profiling is targeting individuals based upon their race. Police officers who engage in this type of policing are wrong, and they will overlook many criminal acts by others.

[25] The Memphis "street crimes" unit was named Scorpion, which was an acronym for Street Crimes Operations to Restore Peace in Our Neighborhoods. "The unit is composed of three teams of about 30 officers whose stated aim is to target violent offenders in areas beset by high crime" (Sainz, 2023).

state of terror,' Bowman said in a fundraising pitch. 'We feel it every day'" (MacDonald, 2023).

That the five police officers charged with Nichols's murder were Black does not refute the racism narrative, argue political and press elites. Black police officers, no less than white police officers, absorb the police culture of anti-Black racism, the argument goes (MacDonald, 2023).

Speculation before any facts are known is not helpful. Those who continue the narrative saying racism exists in this situation without further evidence are engaging in mental contortionism. "The only question should be: what is the actual evidence race affected the use of force? Those who contend racism killed Tyre Nichols have no evidence to back up their claim, so they offer a thought experiment instead: Would the five Memphis police officers have behaved as brutally had Nichols been white? To anti-cop activists, the answer is self-evidently no.

According to Heather MacDonald, "another thought experiment is in order: Did these police officers possess the tactical skill and psychological disposition to conduct any high-risk car stop according to professional standards? Given what is shown in the videos, the answer, even more self-evidently, is no" (MacDonald, 2023). There are times where a simple explanation is best with readily available evidence. The videos of the encounter immediately indicate a lack of discipline on the part of the officers. A probe into the minds of the officers regarding their potential for racial bias, although possibly helpful, could overshadow the true reasons for their actions.

The explanation for the Memphis officers' actions espouses the theory that those Black police officers became infected with white racism and that was the reason why they beat and killed Tyree Nichols. These same, seemingly intelligent, people bypassed Occam's razor: the simplest explanation is usually the best. The five officers involved were out of control, poorly supervised, and they were acting purely on power, control, arrogance, and emotion.

One other aspect of the Memphis case, which is not victim shaming, are the actions of Tyree. His reactions to the ostensibly trained officers ripping him out of the vehicle were completely understandable. It is not a simple task to stay calm and do as an officer is instructing, especially if they are yelling, manhandling, and giving contrary commands. The sympathetic nervous system energizes the fight or flight response, and most citizens don't have experience or training in how to control this reaction. Therefore, citizens will resist by arguing, then fighting, and finally possibly fleeing. Yes, it's easy to tell a citizen to just listen to what a police officer tells you and you will be fine. If it was the only message being delivered regarding police-citizen interactions then, maybe, just maybe, there would be less violent confrontations between police and citizens.

Unfortunately, many minorities have been preached to about police officers being racist and how they're going to beat them down. Minorities begin to believe it when they are told over and over again the police are bad, and cops are out to get them. Maybe citizens would be better served if "The Talk" focused more on their actions rather than what actions police may or may not take. Instilling fear of the police could predispose someone to automatically resisting if confronted by the police, which escalates the police-citizen encounter from the very start.

This is why both parties involved in a police-citizen interaction must respect each other. Deconfliction will not resolve any residual racial practices ingrained within an agency or end the overlooking of racial profiling by some officers, but it could reduce violent encounters between law enforcement officers and citizens if practiced by all.

CHAPTER 7

MENTAL HEALTH CRISIS

"Dispatch, 266."

"Respond to a family member refusing to leave."

This sounds like a routine incident call, which police are dispatched to on a regular basis. There are, however, many nuances to this situation based on local laws related to residency and eviction, which can be worked through once the law enforcement officer arrives on scene. Unfortunately, many times a family member is suffering from some level of mental illness, which is not communicated by the caller to dispatch, or the dispatcher is aware, but they fail to provide the information to the officer. Other times, officers are familiar with the individual and their potential mental state. In either case, when the officers arrive, they have to make a quick assessment whether the person they must ask to leave is mentally stable.

The call I responded to on this particular evening was one where I was not made aware of the mental state of the family member.

When I arrived, I spoke to a woman at the front door who said she wanted her son to leave. I looked past her and could see a very large man, at least 6'3", 250 pounds, in his twenties sitting in a chair in the living room. The woman told me he wasn't right in the head, and he was not allowed at the house. I tried to talk to him through the front door, but he refused to say anything; he just stared back at me. I immediately had the sense it would be a fight if I tried to escort this young man from the house. I called for backup.

Any interaction between police and a citizen suffering from a mental illness could result in a violent encounter: "Police departments say 10 percent of their contact with the public involves a person with mental illness, and those with untreated symptoms account for more than 1 in 4 fatal police shootings" (Walters, 2020).

Police have seen an increase in interactions with people suffering from mental illnesses or mental breakdowns (Abramson, 2021). I am not going to opine on why there might be more people experiencing some sort of mental crisis; it's not in my lane. The focus here is on how law enforcement interacts with people who may be suffering from a diagnosed mental illness or undergoing a mental health episode.

Statistically, there are millions of Americans who suffer from a mental illness at one point or another in their life. These numbers provide a glimpse at how many people face a mental health or substance use challenge, whether we see it or not:

Millions of people in the U.S. are affected by mental illness each year.

- 22.8% of U.S. adults experienced mental illness in 2021 (57.8 million people). This represents 1 in 5 adults.

- 5.5% of U.S. adults experienced serious mental illness in 2021 (14.1 million people). This represents 1 in 20 adults.

- 16.5% of U.S. youth aged 6-17 experienced a mental health disorder in 2016 (7.7 million people).

CHAPTER 7

- 7.6% of U.S. adults experienced a co-occurring substance use disorder and mental illness in 2021 (19.4 million people).

- 47.2% of U.S. adults with mental illness received treatment in 2021.

- 65.4% of U.S. adults with serious mental illness received treatment in 2021 (National Alliance on Mental Illness, 2023).

The above numbers suggest 52.8% of adults in 2021 with a mental disorder did not seek professional help. This opens the door for many law enforcement encounters with individuals who may not think rationally. Law enforcement, in most jurisdictions, retains information related to the prior encounters with citizens who have a history of psychological issues; however, if a citizen is not in the dispatch system, officers could be responding to a potentially dangerous situation without important information. When officers have previously interacted with someone who has mental health issues, they tend to know how to approach the citizen. This knowledge could reinforce the use of the Deconfliction elements before officers arrive on scene. The mental preparation an officer performs enroute to a particular call for service often sets the stage for a positive police-citizen interaction and resolution.

Police officers have multiple possibilities to consider when responding to a call involving a person with a mental illness or someone having a mental health crisis. Excited delirium syndrome[26] (ExDS) is one of the controversial conditions which has been thrust into the spotlight in the past decade. "The characteristic symptoms of ExDS include bizarre and aggressive behavior, shouting, paranoia, panic, violence toward others, unexpected physical strength, and hyperthermia. Throughout the United States and Canada, these cases are most frequently associated with cocaine, methamphetamine, and designer cathinone abuse" (Mash, 2016). Additionally, ExDS "has two

---

[26] As noted in the APA's Position Statement on Police Interactions with Persons with Mental Illness (2017), in a range of crisis situations, law enforcement officers are called as first responders and may find individuals who are agitated, disorganized, and/or behaving erratically. Such behaviors may be due to mental illness, intellectual or developmental disabilities, neurocognitive disorders, substance use, or extreme emotional states. Police responses to calls for behavioral health crises have been known to result in tragic outcomes, including injury or death. The concept of "excited delirium" (also referred to as "excited delirium syndrome (ExDS)") has been invoked in a number of cases to explain or justify injury or death to individuals in police custody, and the term "excited delirium" is disproportionately applied to Black men in police custody. Although the American College of Emergency Physicians has explicitly recognized "excited delirium" as a medical condition, the criteria are unclear, and to date, there have been no rigorous studies validating "excited delirium" as a medical diagnosis. APA has not recognized "excited delirium" as a mental disorder, and it is not included in the Diagnostic and Statistical Manual of Mental Disorders (DSM5). The DSM-5 recognizes Delirium, hyperactive type, but the symptoms of this condition differ in many ways from the symptoms typically attributed to "excited delirium" (e.g., superhuman strength, impervious to pain, etc.). Recent data suggest that persons being detained by the police and described as having "excited delirium" have frequently received medication from emergency medical technicians (EMTs) with the intent to rapidly sedate them. Ketamine, an FDA-approved medication for anesthesia, is often used for this purpose. In some reported cases, it is questionable whether the person identified as having an "excited delirium" actually had any medical condition warranting its use. Many sedating medications used outside of hospital contexts, including ketamine, have significant risks, including respiratory suppression. Supporting respiration may be challenging outside of a hospital setting, where it may require intensive medical oversight or involvement (APA Official Actions Position Statement on Concerns about Use of the Term "Excited Delirium" and Appropriate Medical Management in Out-of-Hospital Contexts, 2020).

main triggers: acute drug use and psychiatric illness" (Sengstock & Curtis, 2022).

Police must always keep personal safety concerns in mind when responding to a mental health related call. When police officers arrive at a call, "Maintaining safety on scene is paramount, which can be supported by a dual response by paramedics and law enforcement officers, [if] the patient is likely to need restraining or sedation" (Sengstock & Curtis, 2022).

While I waited for backup, I tried to talk to the young man through the door, and he told me his mother didn't treat him well, but he was not going to leave. I didn't suspect he had been using any drugs at that time; however, he was still acting too quiet, and I had the sense he could become aggressive at any point if I started giving him orders to leave the house.

Two other officers and a lieutenant arrived as backup. We entered the house, and the young man stood up from his chair. The young man towered over the lieutenant, who, it must be noted, didn't back down. The lieutenant grabbed the young man, and the fight was on, ending up in the front yard. The young man was super strong, and it took all of us to get him secured in handcuffs. We quickly placed him in my patrol car, and I took him to jail for disorderly conduct.

This incident could have gone much worse. It does illustrate how a situation with an unstable or mentally ill person could become violent without warning. The mere presence of law enforcement personnel can excite individuals who already distrust the police. But what's the answer?

There is a wide range of responses to the mental health crisis across the country from sending social workers with paramedics to calls for service involving mentally ill citizens to sending social workers or mental health counselors with police to those calls. A program in Eugene, Oregon, which began 30 years ago, "sends out two people, a medic and a crisis responder, instead of an armed cop" (Walters, 2020). Clinic coordinator Ben Brubaker indicated that the program currently handles 20 percent of the 911 calls at a cost of $2.1 million (Walters, 2020).

This program may not work in every city across the country depending on manning and funding.

Colorado has mental health professionals respond to mental health calls along with police. Cities like Denver and Grand Junction receive about $362,000 a year from a marijuana tax to fund mental health experts (Walters, 2020).

The impact of the latest variations of police and social workers combination has not been comprehensively studied in the United States. Additionally, there are many subtleties to the collaborations between police and mental health professionals and, "many programs are limited in hours or operation or geographical area served" (Balfour et al., 2021). Local authorities may have to think outside the box and adjust these partnerships between police and mental health professionals to accommodate specific requirements of the community.

The test of the collaborations between paramedics coupled with social workers will come when they encounter a citizen experiencing a mental health crisis and that person becomes violent, and someone is gravely injured. Unfortunately, if that situation occurs, it may not be widely reported for obvious biased reasons. Even though the defund the police movement in 2020 has since been dialed back in light of increased violence throughout the country, there are still many advocates for reducing the law enforcement presence within communities.

The prevailing reason for dispatching non-law enforcement to mental health crisis calls for service is that, as indicated above, police can provoke resistance or a violent response through their presence alone. I will discuss actions of law enforcement officers which can contribute to agitating a citizen having a mental health crisis.

In chapters 2 and 3, I explained the force continuum and how officers are taught to gain control of a situation for officer safety. This mindset is typically translated into projecting authority and a command presence manifested by making demands or giving orders. Remember, included in the indicators of ExDS are shouting, aggressive behavior, and violence toward others. So, this is a case of the age-old question: which comes first? Do

CHAPTER 7

police cause ExDS, or is a citizen in the midst of an ExDS episode and then the police are called to the scene? One thing is certain: the combination of a citizen experiencing a mental health crisis who possibly has used some sort of amphetamine and typical law enforcement tactics can lead to death.

The better tactic could be a softer approach when interacting with a citizen who is experiencing a mental health crisis. Yes, this is where the Principles of Deconfliction come in. Yes, it will be difficult, especially for younger officers who may not have had any seasoning to present a calmer attitude in this type of situation. However, presenting a more subdued and friendly manner is not always going to elicit compliance. As my opening story in the prologue demonstrated, a seemingly compliant subject can turn instantly to violence. I tried being disarming in my contact with the subject, and the subject in turn attempted to disarm me.

Absent any readily available data related to mental health professionals responding to calls for service without police assistance, it is difficult to make an assessment regarding the outcomes of those interactions. A clearer picture may occur once there are actual statistics of these interactions as compared to similar situations involving solely the police. Every confrontation would have to be reviewed independently through any report generated. Therein lies the problem. The report may lack important details depending on the author such as the exact behavior of an individual before, during, and after either police or non-police contact the person having the mental health crisis. This might make a great thesis for some promising doctoral candidate.

The unfortunate result of the politicization of citizens dying at the hands of police while experiencing a mental health crisis was the reduction of the police force, which reduces the safety of an entire community. These horrific incidents have caused a national dialogue about possible solutions. One such possible remedy, which has recently been suggested, is to bring back state-run mental health facilities. There have been numerous books written about the evils and inhumane conditions at some state psychiatric hospitals. Currently, there are only a handful of psychiatric hospitals located in the United States.[27] Even if state mental health facilities are the answer, a potential problem remains. If the family of someone suffering from a mental illness does not come forward until the family member becomes aggressive or violent, the police, or social worker, or mental health professional will still have to interact with the individual.

There is no perfect antidote, or one size fits all procedure for authorities to resolve a situation peacefully when a citizen is having a mental health crisis, even if the citizen does all they can in order to provoke violence. Those suffering from a mental illness who then experience a mental health crisis need law enforcement and mental health professionals to work together to find best practices for interacting with those citizens.

---

[27] "The 20th century contains dramatic changes in the roles played by psychiatric hospitals. From 1900 to 1955, the peak year-end census in state and county hospitals, public psychiatric hospitals were provided minimal resources to meet the needs of huge patient populations. Subsequently, as these hospitals were progressively eviscerated, the hospitals and those who worked there were vilified, perhaps as a way to assuage the guilt of what happened to their former residents." (Geller, 2019)

CHAPTER 8

TRAINING EVOLUTION

"Foot pursuit!"

When I started with the Charleston, South Carolina, City Police, I was involved in my first foot pursuit while still going through field training. One night, several teenagers broke into a pawn shop, stole a few mini-motorcycles, and were careening through the local neighborhood. I was driving a marked patrol vehicle with Trey, my Field Training Officer (FTO), who was calling out what street to turn on to try and locate the juveniles. We arrived in the area and immediately saw the kids bombing down the street and fleeing the scene. We approached an intersection, and one of the kids fell off the stolen motorcycle as he rounded the corner. Trey screamed, "Stop!" and then he bailed out of the car to grab the young man who had fallen. I saw another juvenile running along the sidewalk after he jumped off the motorbike he was riding, so I stepped on the gas to catch up. The young man, looking back as he ran, turned the corner, and as I approached him, engine revving, he quickly stopped and doubled back.

Damn it! Nice move.

I threw the car in reverse, whipped the steering wheel, gunned the throttle, and chased after him. This was my first pursuit. I was not going to let him get away.

The juvenile looked over his shoulder to see me coming down the street, so he ran between two houses. It was my turn to bail out of the car. I chased the young man around the house and watched as he jumped a 3-foot fence to an adjacent yard. I kept him in my sights as I climbed over the fence, and just as I landed, I noticed a clothesline in the middle of the yard. A few seconds later, the juvenile ran straight into the clothesline, which was around chest height, and in cartoon fashion, his feet came out from under him, and in an instant, he was flat on his back. I could barely control my laughter as I rolled him over to put him in handcuffs.

There was no training at the South Carolina Criminal Justice Academy which would have prepared me for that foot pursuit. Police are taught ways to interact with citizens who are complying and not complying with commands, and then the methods of control progresses from there as discussed in earlier chapters. Law enforcement training focuses on not violating the guaranteed rights of citizens outlined by the U.S. Constitution, which includes training on the use of force and the reasonableness of the force used by officers.[28]

Every career field, job, or profession evolves and develops new policies and procedures based upon situations which have occurred. New policies are typically enacted because someone did something stupid or their actions prompted a civil lawsuit. In law enforcement, those new policies are usually dubbed the "Insert Name of Officer Who Screwed Up Here" policy. Law

---

[28] The Fourth Amendment "reasonableness" inquiry is whether the officers' actions are "objectively reasonable" in light of the facts and circumstances confronting them, without regard to their underlying intent or motivation. The "reasonableness" of a particular use of force must be judged from the perspective of a reasonable officer on the scene, and its calculus must embody an allowance for the fact that police officers are often forced to make split- second decisions about the amount of force necessary in a particular situation. Pp. 490 U. S. 396-397 (US Supreme Court, 1989).

CHAPTER 8

enforcement is notorious for dramatically overreacting. Many of those overreactions are traced back to some dubious legal advice meant to protect the agency and not necessarily advance the standard operating procedures of law enforcement.

New training in law enforcement is generally spurred by analysis of incidents resulting in death or serious injury to law enforcement personnel or citizens. I call this the natural evolution of training as opposed to the forced imposition of new tactics. To illustrate this point, I will review a few of the tactical changes I have experienced throughout my career.

I heard that, in the old days, shooting qualifications had officers fire two rounds and then holster.

The act of immediately holstering after shooting the required number of rounds created the muscle memory of putting your weapon away after firing those shots. Any potential issues come to mind? The problem arose when, in real-life gun battles, officers exchanged gunfire with a subject and holstered their weapon after firing only two rounds regardless of whether the threat was stopped. This automatic muscle memory response put officers' lives at risk as well as innocent bystanders. Training evolved into officers assessing the threat to determine if there was any more possible danger before making the conscious decision to holster their weapon. The assessment was designed to force the officer to look around, left, and right to break the tunnel vision typically experienced by everyone involved in an extremely violent situation.

Firearms instructors for the Criminal Investigator Training Program (CITP) at the Federal Law Enforcement Training Centers (FLETC) in Georgia taught us to "offline" or sidestep as we drew our weapons to shoot the course of fire. I have also been told by former officers from local agencies that they were taught to move off the kill zone or "X" after firing a few rounds. The thinking is once the officer shoots, the subject is more likely to fire back at the last position where the officer was as indicated by the flash coming from the muzzle of the gun.

When reviewing footage of officer-involved shooting videos where the officer is injured or killed, the prevailing tactic used by the bad guy is moving while shooting and many times charging right at the officer. Law enforcement firearms training may need more changes to keep up with actions of would-be criminals. Nevertheless, safety first often hampers real world training. If firearms training became more realistic to help prepare officers for what they may encounter on duty, the number of accidents or deaths could dramatically rise, and police agencies could face extensive adverse legal actions if firearms training accidents were more prolific.

So-called routine traffic stops are anything but routine. Traffic stops, next to domestic violence calls, are some of the most dangerous actions police officers can perform. There was a shift from driver-side approaches when conducting traffic stops to a passenger-side approach during my law enforcement career. As it turns out, the passenger side provides officers with a better view inside the vehicle and an enhanced view of the driver's movements. This change in tactic was another natural evolution after many officers were shot walking up to the driver's side of a vehicle, which allowed the driver to conceal a weapon more easily and fire upon the officer more quickly.

Another tactical change related to offer safety I personally experienced was the aptly named "surround and callout." Special Weapons and Tactics (SWAT) teams use this method of arresting a subject more often now as opposed to marching up to the front door, knocking, ramming down the door, and then rushing in. This technique is utilized especially if the subject is known to have weapons. A SWAT team can form a perimeter around a residence and then pull up to the front door with an armored vehicle to use a loudspeaker to call the subject out. Tear gas can also be deployed into the residence to force the subject to surrender. The team may eventually have to break down the door and enter, but it's safer to give a subject an opportunity to exit without any violent incident occurring. I am not certain who coined this phrase, but possibly it was thought up after a long SWAT operation of the surround and call out was over. SWAT is also affectionately known as "Sit Wait and Talk." As a former sniper on the Charleston County Sheriff's Office SWAT

CHAPTER 8

team, "Sit Wait and Talk" was perfectly fine with me. Respect to those door kickers out there.

Law enforcement must change with the times. Gone are the days when people immediately complied with a police officer's commands. Citizens expect more from police during a police-citizen encounter to include more respect, more detailed explanations as to why they are being contacted, more understanding, and more empathy. These expectations are warranted and should be heeded. Deconfliction could start a trend of civil interactions between law enforcement and citizens.

We can also debate whether citizens should demand answers in the middle of an interaction about why an officer is asking or telling them to do something. I think training should reflect this new dynamic between police and citizens to a certain degree. However, I learned in my time on the street that it's best not to get into an argument with someone when attempting to control a situation. By following the Deconfliction Principles, an officer can acknowledge the problem and confront those negative feelings while actively listening to the citizen, and then carefully choose words to succinctly answer the citizen's concerns.

Training changes can also be forced. What is forced tends not to become fully vetted for many years. One of those changes, in my humble opinion, was de-escalation training. How predictable was that?

The forerunner to de-escalation was verbal judo. Both verbal judo and de-escalation are reactive methods of gaining compliance from a citizen. The well-known axiom "Reaction is always slower than action" means that implementing a response to an act is already starting behind the curve.

Yes, this book does promote Deconfliction, which is more of a mindset rather than a method, but throughout my experience, it's more productive to operate on the complete-person concept. An officer who demonstrates a combative demeanor but then must use de-escalation to defuse a situation is far less effective than an officer who practices the Deconfliction Principles from the very start of a citizen interaction. What's that saying about getting more flies with honey?

Law enforcement as a profession and officers are infamous for being resistant to change and slow to implement any new tactics unless forced. From my experience, some reasons behind the slow to change attitude come from command level officials who are removed from daily police operations and don't have the desire to entertain new ideas or do have the arrogance of knowing what's best.

There are some very progressive police chiefs and sheriffs in the country who are always looking for the best practices and the best equipment. Funding is always an issue for training and newer tools for officers. Another issue is deciding what training is the most advantageous for a particular agency. What might be necessary training for the Los Angeles Police Department may not be essential for officers in a small town in rural America. However, the same police agency in a small town in rural America may need more equipment in their vehicles than the officers in Los Angeles, considering L.A. has many more officers per square mile than an agency in Wyoming or Montana.

The law enforcement industrial complex includes academia as well. One might be surprised at how many professors with a PhD in criminal justice have never spent any significant time walking in the boots of law enforcement officers. Many of these same doctors are responsible for the basis and theory for much of the training actual police officers receive. The good news is that more police officers are going back to school to receive their doctorate in criminal justice. The possibility of more insightful training becomes more real when those with true law enforcement experience enter the academic arena.

Training in law enforcement relies on conducting practical exercises to give future officers a frame of reference and experience in handling various situations. The more time devoted to practical, true to life training, which incorporates classroom legal instruction, could be the best method of raising the professionalism bar in law enforcement. Practical exercises have gone through a theoretical basis change which I have personally witnessed.

CHAPTER 8

The conceptual foundation for including realistic exercises into law enforcement training 20 plus years ago was to evaluate how recruits responded to scenarios and make corrections as necessary. Many of those scenes included shoot or don't shoot scenarios which are mainly focused on the thought process and observation skills necessary to determine whether the officer should have used deadly force. This type of training could leave new officers fearful that every person they encounter may have a weapon and try to use it against them. It is good officer safety practice to be prepared; however, this fear could lead officers to act on muscle memory without completely thinking through a situation.

A real incident to illustrate this thought occurred in Texas in October of 2019. Officers with the Fort Worth Police Department were dispatched around 2:25 a.m. to check on an open door at a residence. A neighbor called the police because he noticed the door to the residence had been open since around 10 p.m., and he was concerned about the woman who lived there. One of the officers who responded had been with the department since April of 2018. When the officers arrived, "they thought the house might have been burglarized and quietly moved into the fenced-off backyard looking for signs of forced entry" (News, 2022).[29] The officer involved in the shooting was "peering inside

---

[29] I would have most likely knocked on the front door and announced, "Police" before checking around the residence if called to check the welfare of a resident where the caller indicated a door was open. Not to second guess the actions of the Fort Worth Officers, but if they could have articulated how the front door looked like it had been forced open, then maybe checking around the residence would have been justified. In my own experience, I was called to a similar situation where a neighbor noticed an open door which was normally closed. The difference in my incident was it was in the middle of the day. Another officer and I arrived, and seeing the front door standing open, we knocked and announced our presence. The other officer moved inside toward the kitchen as I watched the stairs. We had our weapons out according to protocol. I continued to call out "Police" as I looked up the stairwell to the second floor, and suddenly, a young boy about 6 years old appeared at the top of the stairs. I exhaled and quickly lowered my weapon. It was a scary set of circumstances early in my career.

a window using a flashlight, spotting someone inside standing near a window and telling her, 'Put your hands up—show me your hands,' before shooting seconds later" (Romero, 2019). The officer was charged with homicide, and in 2022, he was convicted of manslaughter with a 12-year sentence (Jefferson, 2022).

Admittedly, I don't have any information regarding the training the Fort Worth Officer received or any knowledge of his performance during any type of field training. People want a "one size fits all" explanation for why he shot the victim through the window. Many in the media pointed to the fact the officer was white, and the victim was Black as the reason behind the shooting. I would suggest a different explanation.

Muscle memory or more precisely, "brain motor skills memory," could explain why the Fort Worth Officer pulled the trigger without thinking (Udaipurwala, 2021).[30] Consider the number of tasks you perform every day without really thinking. Ask yourself how many times you have driven to work or the supermarket and once you arrived you really couldn't remember the trip. This is muscle memory in action.

We do tasks everyday with little thought because we do them so many times that conscious effort isn't completely necessary. This is called muscle memory. The training law enforcement officers receive amounts to developing their brain's motor memory. Training consists of placing officers in realistic situations where the person may have a weapon, and when a weapon, like a gun, is observed, the officer shoots to eliminate

---

[30] If you ask a well-read non-scientist, they'll give you an answer similar to the one above. Muscle memory, they'll say, is when your brain has learnt a motor task so well that you can perform the task without conscious effort. The most relatable example is riding a bike. To successfully ride a bike, you must do several things at once. You need to keep your posture upright in a way that keeps your center of balance, your legs need to rotate the pedals to get the wheels moving, and you need to maneuver the handles with your arms. All this requires many simultaneous muscle movements to coordinate and puts your senses in overdrive. To coordinate these muscles, parts of the brain involved in motor movement, such as the cerebellum and motor cortices, are activated to move your muscles. These regions have neuronal pathways that allow us to perform complex motor tasks. (Udaipurwala, 2021)

the threat. Do you see the problem with this type of training? Repeatedly, those scenarios are coupled with the person with the gun making some sort of threat, which again is not always the case. The woman in Texas didn't have time to say a word.

An improvement to realistic training couples the brain's motor memory with the requirement to articulate an individual's actions after the scenario is over. Instructors at FLETC called this process "creating files." The first part of creating those files is having the experience of interacting with someone who does not comply with commands and then acts aggressively whether by balling their fists up, picking up a weapon like a hammer, or producing a firearm.

The second half of the training incorporates an articulation session once the scene is completed, which forces law enforcement trainees to explain their actions. Law enforcement officers must develop the necessary observation skills to describe why they did what they did when interacting with the roleplayer. This trains the officer to consciously think about the situation in its totality using the Graham factors.[31]

Will this new method of training avoid situations like in Fort Worth, Texas? It must be considered that situations in law enforcement can occur in split seconds, and law enforcement officers have the same fears as ordinary citizens. Officers want to make it home to their families at the end of their shift just as much as citizens[32] don't want officers to cause them harm. Training must continue to evolve to reduce injuries and death to both police and citizens.

Effective communication between police and citizens is very necessary for keeping all parties involved in an interaction calm,

---

[31] The [Supreme] Court requires careful attention to the facts and circumstance of each case, including the severity of the crime at issue, whether the suspect poses an immediate threat to the safety of the officers or others, and whether the suspect is actively resisting arrest or attempting to evade arrest by flight (Ross, 2002).

[32] It must be noted there is a criminal element out there who have targeted police. These are not the "citizens" being referred to here.

respectful, and free from violent actions. Deconfliction seeks to not only develop a different mindset for law enforcement officers but to impart the same approach to citizens who find themselves involved in an interaction or confrontation with police.

The next chapter will explore some of the issues arising between citizens and police from the perspective of the actions of the citizen. The goal of the discussion is to assist in lowering the starting temperature when police-citizen encounters occur.

CHAPTER 9

CITIZEN DUTY
(DON'T BECOME A STATISTIC)

A long tone sounds over the police radio.

"Dispatch to all west units, there is a robbery in progress at the First Citizens Bank in Hollywood. Units responding acknowledge."

"266 in route."

I threw on the lights and siren of my patrol car and hauled ass south on highway 17. As we were responding, dispatch started to give out further information over the radio which sounded like the suspect was being followed by a citizen. Dispatch was relaying information from a call-taker who was relaying information from someone on the phone who was talking to another person. It was a very bad game of telephone.

Sound confusing? It was. I told dispatch to tell the person who was on the phone to meet me at a local fire station. I arrived at the station, and minutes later, a couple pulled up next to me. The man said his brother was following the robbery suspect and had called him rather than 911. The man I was with then called 911 and was acting as middleman for his brother who was still following the suspect. Still with me? I took the phone and talked directly to the man following the suspect and relayed his location over my police radio to the officers looking for the suspect. This took the tag team relay between the two brothers out of the loop as well as dispatch, which allowed for real-time communication with the other deputies who were attempting to locate the suspect of the bank robbery.

The suspect stopped at a residence. Minutes later, deputies arrived at the location, and eventually, the robber was apprehended. The bank robbery incident is a great example of citizens assisting the police.

Do citizens have a duty to act in a certain way when they interact with or are confronted by the police?

In fact, they do. By law, citizens must provide their license, registration, and insurance when police pull them over while driving. Citizens, by law, must not obstruct officers from performing their duties. Additionally, citizens are required to comply with all lawful orders by police. However, the time to determine if an order is lawful is not in the heat of the encounter. In the name of civility, everyone would be better served if objections and opposition to specific police orders were questioned and resolved through police channels or the courts.

The last statement regarding complying with lawful orders is probably the most important and the foundation of a peaceful citizen-police interaction. Compliance does not equate to acquiescence.

Before I go further, I must make it crystal clear in no way, shape, or form am I intending to fully blame a citizen for any unprofessional actions by a law enforcement officer. It's my belief there is generally plenty of blame to go around when a situation goes awry.

That being written, I would like to suggest citizens as well as officers need to "deconflict" a situation. I have a few suggestions for citizens which could keep them safe and free from becoming a statistic when they have contact with a law enforcement officer.

CHAPTER 9

As a former law enforcement officer, the best advice I can provide to any citizen who is approached by a police officer is to be polite and avoid "roadside activism." What do I mean by "roadside activism"? If you believe an officer is stopping you for no reason, pleading your case through protest on the side of the road is generally not effective. I encourage citizens to ask the officer why they have been pulled over or why the officer has contacted them. This is best performed in a polite, non-accusatory way. If the officer does not present a clear reason, just make note of it if you are inclined to make a formal complaint later and move on with what the officer is asking you for or to do. Most police officers wear body cameras, so rest assured if you see one, it's probably recording the incident. A citizen is more than welcome to record an encounter on their phone, but it is advisable to just passively record the incident and don't play commentator on the video thinking you will get more likes once you post it on social media. This only further distracts and is not part of the Deconfliction Principles. More on this later in the chapter.

There could be a downside to asking questions. When I conducted a traffic stop when I was a patrol officer, the first question I normally asked was, "Do you know why I pulled you over." Now, if the person said, "Yes sir, I was probably going a little too fast." Or "Yes, I may have rolled through a stop sign." I would more than likely just give them a warning. If the driver admitted to committing a moving violation, it told me they were at least paying some attention to their own driving. If the person said they had no idea why I pulled them over, it would make me more concerned about their driving abilities and whether they were actually focused on driving, and I would be more inclined to issue a citation.

Remember, police are trained to control a situation through officer presence, then verbal commands. If you verbally attack an officer with accusations from the very start of the encounter, the officer, being human, will initially become defensive, unless of course he is practicing Deconfliction. However, even if the officer initially does not escalate the situation, but the citizen continues to become more aggressive or louder in their protesting, the officer will draw upon his training and attempt to control the situation. Unfortunately, this is the point where things could begin to go wrong.

There are plenty of videos out there showing the interaction between citizens and police not only from body cameras worn by officers but from citizens. Some of those videos were recorded by citizens in direct contact with police, and others are videos captured by onlookers. I will first discuss videos created by those citizens directly involved in the encounter.

I encourage every citizen, as mentioned above, to record their interaction with the police if it makes them feel safer. Sometimes the act of playing for the camera can escalate the situation. The online activism practiced today can hype a situation far beyond what could have been an innocuous citizen and police encounter. Additionally, any preconceived notion regarding the reason for the stop or possible implied bias can also factor into how a citizen reacts, which in turn can increase the tension.

My suggestion, if you want to record the incident even though the officer is wearing a body camera, which may not be activated, is to passively produce the video without adding commentary to the camera. Always remember that the recording not only captures the actions of the officer but will also capture your actions as well.

The second type of videos out there on the web are those captured by onlookers. These usually receive the most scrutiny. Again, I encourage spectators to record interactions between citizens and police they are witnessing but with the caveat of staying a disinterested observer.

What is a disinterested observer? This is someone who records the events without interjecting their thoughts, opinions, or distracting officers from performing their duties. Officers are trained to be aware of their surroundings (the other situational awareness) when they are in the process of attempting to control a suspect. The situation could become more volatile if a bystander begins to voice concerns about what they believe is excessive force or ill treatment of the citizen by the officer.

CHAPTER 9

The officer could become concerned that an onlooker, who is recording the scene, may become aggressive toward the officer, which then causes the officer to overlook the health and safety of the person they are in the process of apprehending.

There are many examples of observers interjecting various comments or otherwise becoming involved in a citizen and police confrontation when they don't have any personal stake in the situation.

I will now deliver some thoughts on an interaction which occurred recently between the citizens who witnessed a horrific and dishonorable incident between several police and one man. George Floyd died while primarily in the hands of Derek Chauvin, a Minneapolis, Minnesota, police officer.

First, a disclaimer: I will in no way suggest, imply, or outright say the citizens who witnessed and recorded the Floyd incident directly caused or in any deliberate way contributed to his death. This chapter is about the way in which citizens interact with the police and some ideas about how it could be improved. The Deconfliction Principles don't necessarily apply to onlookers because of their very nature, except for maybe situational awareness. Onlookers are not always privy to all of the facts surrounding the incident they are observing, and if they were present for the entire encounter, they are probably not the main focus of the officer.

As I described above, officers are in a heightened state of awareness when they have to use force to control a citizen. The higher state of alert can translate into a defensive posture. Officers will focus on a perceived threat the intervening citizen may pose to their safety; therefore, the intervening citizen may potentially inadvertently prolong the use of force against the citizen the police are trying to control and place under arrest. Think of it this way: If you are arguing with someone, and another person you don't know walks up and starts to yell you are doing something wrong, how would you react?

It is understandable how the people witnessing the actions of the police against George Floyd were horrified by what they saw. Moreover, it was more than reasonable for those same people to want to do something to help. Unfortunately, what they were doing may have extended the time the police held Mr. Floyd down without checking on his welfare.

The law enforcement officer mentality and thought process must be explored to understand how confronting officers could have extended the time before officers addressed the health of Mr. Floyd. As discussed in chapter three, officers are trained to control a scene. When unknown individuals approach officers performing their duties, they can become protective. If you are not known to an officer, they are more likely to resist your involvement, especially if you are criticizing their actions. If an officer is challenged, they may not want to acknowledge what they are doing could be improper as it could show weakness or guilt. Officers face more liability in today's society, which overall assists in ridding agencies of bad officers, but it also has the effect of officers being less ready to admit mistakes. Officers could feel more open to being named in a personal lawsuit if they capitulate to the demands of a crowd.

One of the witnesses voicing their concern about the treatment of Mr. Floyd was apparently a Minneapolis firefighter. The firefighter did not appear to offer any identification to confirm this assertion, and the witness was not wearing any type of firefighter uniform. The apparent firefighter and a second witness did call 911, but from the transcripts, it appears those calls were placed after Mr. Floyd was deceased. The Minneapolis police "released two 911 transcripts from May 25, 2020. One transcript was from an unidentified off-duty firefighter who witnessed Floyd's death:

'I literally watched police officers not take a pulse and not do anything to save a man, and I am a first responder myself, and I literally have it on video camera. ... I just happened to be on a walk so, this dude, this, they f*****g killed him,' the firefighter told dispatchers..." (Vera & Meilhan, 2020).

The other caller was also unidentified and mentioned how an officer "'pretty much just killed this guy that wasn't resisting arrest.' That caller then requested to speak to a supervisor at the Minneapolis 3rd Precinct" (Vera & Meilhan, 2020).

CHAPTER 9

The language used in this phone call seems to indicate that Mr. Floyd was already deceased. Would it have been better if multiple witnesses called 911 to report the incident? [33]

A dispatcher watched the incident on surveillance cameras, which happened to catch the incident, and thought a supervisor should be notified. The dispatcher called a patrol supervisor and said, "You can call me a snitch if you want to, but we have the cameras up for 320's call ... I don't know if they had to use force or not, but they got something out of the back of the squad, and all of them sat on this man, so I don't know if they needed you or not, but they haven't said anything to me yet" (Vera & Meilhan, 2020). The supervisor did respond; however, it was approximately 15 minutes before the sergeant arrived on scene (Elfrink, 2020).

If numerous calls about the situation flowed into 911, the dispatcher would have most likely relayed this information to the sergeant, which could have prompted a faster response to the scene or even an attempt to raise the officers involved in the incident on the radio.

Although the onlookers had noble intentions, their efforts to save Mr. Floyd may have been better served by flooding 911 with calls conveying the disturbing details being witnessed.

Every citizen makes their own decision whether they want to step in and be involved in a situation they are witnessing. The best course of action should be carefully considered if a citizen does choose to intervene in a police action. The most helpful assistance could simply be calling 911, giving specific details of the incident as it is occurring, and being a good witness.

If citizens also adopt the Deconfliction Principles and accept they have a duty and a role to play when encountered by the police, there is a greater likelihood the interaction will not become violent, thereby reducing the possibility of the citizen being a statistic.

---

[33] In my law enforcement experience, the more calls we received about gun shots in a specific area, the more legitimate the call seemed, which in turn stepped up our response to the scene.

CHAPTER 10

REIMAGINE POLICING

It is always with the best intentions that the worst work is done."

– Oscar Wilde

Police reimagined. Best intentions?
The "Reimagine Police" initiative has been discussed, argued, and touted with no clarity along with "defund the police." How exactly would taking money away from police departments impact the way police interact with citizens? This narrative seems like parents taking away the allowance of all their children because one of them did something terrible. A grand attempt at peer pressure in the public sector maybe.

In the summer of 2020, the rally cry, among others, was "defund the police." Lawmakers were pressured to cut police funds and reinvest the money in services. The reformed budgets of 2021 saw a redistribution of law enforcement money to housing, mental health programs, food access, and other programs (Levin, 2021). One city, Austin, Texas, is an example of such a city diverting funds away from the police department as stated by one city leader, "We are showing the country how reinvestments from the police budget can actually make many people's lives so much better and safer," said Gregorio Casar, a councilmember in Austin, Texas, who helped pass a major cut to the city's law enforcement budget and is now reallocating those dollars to housing programs (Levin, 2021).

Additionally, "more than 20 major cities have reduced their police budgets in some form, an unprecedented trend, though the scale and circumstances vary dramatically. The activists who have long campaigned to take money from US police are now fighting to ensure that the initial cuts are only the start—and that a growing backlash from law enforcement, elected officials and some community groups does not derail their progress" (Levin, 2021). Flash forward several years and that trend reversed. Due to rising violent crime, "some cities across the nation that previously cut police funding are reconsidering their stance" (McIntire & Bowens, 2023). Unfortunately, the damage was done, and it may take several years before police agencies are back to full staffing.

An online search for the correlation between spending on law enforcement and crime rates is mired in a morass of charts, statistics, quantum physics theory, and explanations of how spending on police in a community has never shown to have an inverse relationship to crime rates. It is important to scrutinize the language used when reading reports or articles and even in this book. One word could make all the difference. Let's look at an example from *The Washington Post*. The article by Philip Bump is titled, "Over the past 60 years, more spending on police hasn't necessarily meant less crime." Bump suggests there is no connection between the amount of money spent on police and the reduction of crime. Bump wrote the following: "Intuitively, one might worry reducing police spending would lead to a spike in crime. A review of spending on state and local police over the past 60 years, though, shows no correlation nationally between spending and crime rates" (Bump, 2020). Can you spot the one word skewing the entire statement? The spending of state and local departments may have an impact on state and local crime statistics but tying the spending to "national" crime rates seems

CHAPTER 10

disingenuous. Ponder that for a moment and draw your own conclusions.

Maybe it's me, but if there were more police on the streets, then wouldn't it stand to reason there would be more arrests, hence higher crime rates? This is just a question to ponder.

A search of the number of crimes which go unreported is staggering. Author Malcom Gladwell in *The Tipping Point* suggested crime, the increase and dramatic decrease, could be likened to an epidemic. At some point, the crime rate, specifically in New Your City, tipped and plummeted. The explanation for the sudden drop in crime was "The New York City police will tell you that what happened in New York was that the city's policing strategies dramatically improved. Criminologists point to the decline of the crack trade and the aging of the population. Economists, meanwhile, say that the gradual improvement in the city's economy over the course of the 1990s had the effect of employing those who might otherwise have become criminals" (Gladwell, 2000). There can be many factors and theories as to why crime rates are reducing; however, one aspect is certain, if there aren't police to arrest criminals their actions will most often go unchecked.

In 1982, James Q. Wilson and George Kelling[34] proposed the "Broken Windows Theory." The broken windows theory was a metaphor linking crime and the increases in crime to the disrepair of a community. The theory became a staple in the 1990s. The theory is based upon the notion that a small number of individuals commit the majority of crimes and if those individuals are arrested for minor infractions like turnstile jumping or shoplifting more major crimes like robbery will be reduced.

The Broken Windows Theory had an enormous impact on police policy throughout the 1990s and remained influential into the 21st century. Perhaps the most notable application of

---

[34] James Q. Wilson is Shattuck Professor of Government at Harvard and author of *Thinking About Crime*. George L. Kelling, formerly director of the evaluation field staff of the Police foundation, is currently a research fellow at the John F Kennedy School of Government Harvard (Wilson & Kelling, 1982).

the theory was in New York City under the direction of Police Commissioner William Bratton. He and others were convinced that the aggressive order-maintenance practices of the New York City Police Department were responsible for the dramatic decrease in crime rates within the city during the 1990s. Bratton began translating the theory into practice as the chief of New York City's transit police from 1990 to 1992. Squads of plainclothes officers were assigned to catch turnstile jumpers, and as arrests for misdemeanors increased, subway crimes of all kinds decreased dramatically (McKee, 2024). Law enforcement agencies need to return to this type of policing as it has been effective in the past to the overall reduction of criminal activity.

Reality didn't take long to rear its ugly head. Defunding departments did actually have consequences. It affected urban communities the most, culminating in much higher crime rates and longer police response times.[35]

Let's revisit Austin, Texas, and a neighborhood called East Town Lake. In 2021, Rendon Delgado, the president of the neighborhood association, agreed with the idea of police reform. However, "Thirteen months later, as her neighbors discuss arming themselves and installing web cameras and security systems, the Hispanic mother of two believes her worry turned to reality. She said community-based officers who used to be on hand to help address crime and quality of life issues—such as drug dealing, public intoxication, and noise complaints—are now too busy responding to more urgent matters. 'We're suffering out here,' she said. 'We don't have the police here doing what they need to do to keep us safe'" (Plohetski, 2021). This is but one example of a mother's outcry for more police assistance. There are always real consequences to the best intentions, and routinely it affects the most vulnerable among us.

---

[35] Higher crime rates can't be totally contributed to fewer police. During this time, local prosecutors were refusing to press charges for so-called minor crimes, which allowed repeat offenders out of jail to continue to commit crimes. Moreover, bail reform in some cities released repeat offenders out of jail on no bond, again allowing them to continue to terrorize the community.

CHAPTER 10

There are a host of other articles in the *Austin American-Statesman* related to defunding the Austin police and crime rates. I encourage everyone who is interested to do a deep dive, and I want to stress I am not singling out Austin, Texas, for any particular reason other than "Austin's cuts, which amounted to about one-third of its police department's 2020 budget, were the largest in the nation" (Mulder, 2021). Citizens of every city should be concerned about their safety and security as it effects the quality of life. I'm not suggesting you spend every waking moment reviewing the policing practices of your community, but, if necessary, voice your concerns publicly or privately through your vote. It's part of your civic duty.

The catchphrase "Police Reimagined" is certainly clever. In true American fashion, when the call went out to do something, the real response to the question of what the objective was should have been to quote Matt Graver in Sicario, "to dramatically overreact." A more cautious approach might have been the better route than trying to overhaul policing from scratch. Incremental changes typically work better in the long run.

What exactly does police reimagined or reimaging policing actually mean?

Reimagine policing and police reform have different meanings to people all over the globe, making it hard to find mutually agreed upon solutions, ideas, and evidence-based approaches. In the wake of some very concerning excessive use of force by a few police officers in a short period of time, along with the video of one being shown over and over again on the news, there was a call for reimagining policing coupled with defunding the police. Reimagining policing seems to be diametrically opposed to the notion of defunding police.

If changes in how the police operate are the intended end result, then it stands to reason more money for training could be needed. "Some suggest incidents of excessive force are the result of a few 'bad apples,' while others argue that the role of the police is structurally unjust and should be deconstructed, either through defunding or abolishing traditional law enforcement" (Green et al., 2022). Both the defunding and deconstructed camps never really offer a solution. Law enforcement agencies and communities are left to make their own adjustments after the political dust has cleared.

Policing in the United States is mostly local or decentralized; therefore, "enacting uniform reform strategies across nearly 18,000 police departments poses a significant challenge" (Green et al., 2022). Could a more significant strategy be to allow individual departments to access the best course of action to ensure their officers are engaging with the public in the most professional manner?

One potential police reform centers around the concept of procedural justice. The procedural justice framework "is comprised of four components, including: Treating citizens with dignity. Transparency in police action. Giving citizens a voice during encounters. Impartiality in decision-making" (Green et al., 2022). Continuing, "Studies find that when citizens view police as respectful, they are more likely to have positive attitudes toward the police and comply with the law" (Green et al., 2022). These are broad suggestions to improve the interaction between police and citizens. The how to implement these general ideas is still open to practical recommendations.

The first and third component of procedural justice have been discussed in the book *Deconfliction* written by yours truly, which if you have been reading closely, you recognized. Emilee Green (2022) in "The Effectiveness and Implications of Police Reform: A Review of the Literature" goes on to discuss de-escalation training, indicating that "de-escalation training focuses on using verbal and non-verbal communication techniques to reduce a threat, allowing for more time to consider the routes of action or resources to resolve a situation. Proponents suggest that when properly trained, officers can de-escalate a potentially volatile situation with less risk of injury to both the officer and citizen." Ultimately, Emilee Green states, "A recent report found of the nation's 100 largest city police departments, only 56 require officers to attempt to de-escalate situations prior to using force" (Green et al., 2022). De-escalation techniques are still an important training focus for police; however, if the

CHAPTER 10

Deconfliction Principles were taught and utilized an encounter between the police and a citizen may never rise to the level of needing to lower the temperature. This reminds me of when Noah built the ark, before the rain.

Perhaps a change in mindset of police is far better than merely a "policy" requiring officers to de-escalate a situation prior to using force. And as if on cue, here comes Deconfliction and the Deconfliction Principles. De-escalation is the tactic, but more importantly, the Deconfliction Principles are the tools. Changing behaviors starts with changing the thought process (said someone, I'm sure).

With respect to reimagining police, this next definition is from *My Brother's Keeper Alliance:* "The Reimagining Policing Pledge is a call for mayors and local officials to review and reform use of force policies, redefine public safety, and combat systemic racism within law enforcement" (Foundation, n.d.). This proposal again offers little in the way of substance and provides more broad general concepts.

The last police reimagined concept I will present comes from the chief of the Charlotte-Mecklenburg Police Department. Chief Jennings, in June of 2020, "had an epiphany: Adopting the hospitality industry's customer service approach could significantly enhance the CMPD's services and community relations" (Policing Reimagined as Customer Service, 2022). I give the Chief credit for at least proffering a course of action. However, policing is not exactly a customer service job.

Not to undermine Chief Jennings, but back in 2006, the new chief of the Charleston City (South Carolina) Police Department directed officers to attend customer service training presented to other Charleston City employees. It did not go well.

Customer service presumes showing deference to the customer as in "the customer is always right." In law enforcement, the customer is not always right. The concept of customer service is rooted in police being attentive to the needs of citizens and treating them with respect. However, police will always need to maintain some semblance of order during an interaction with a citizen. This is the basis of being an authority figure.

What is needed is a way to retain a position or authority while respecting the citizen. The Deconfliction Principles embody serving the customer model without having to relinquish control to the citizen. When the citizen is drawn into the encounter as an active participant, then there is no need for control. Let's be realistic: unless you are a victim of a crime, no one really wants to be confronted by the police.

But just imagine if you are confronted by an officer, and the officer is calm, direct, polite, and fully aware you are concerned as to why they are talking to you. The officer explains exactly why you are being approached, listens to your questions, and provides full and complete answers. Even if the scenario ended with you facing a traffic citation, would you be more upset about committing the infraction or how you were treated by the officer?

Perhaps the old police motto of "Protect and Serve" should be reformed as well. A less beholden maxim would be "Assist and Enforce." After all, it is the function of the police to assist citizens as needed and to enforce the law. The "serve" part many times was used, in my experience, to justify the very helpful "I pay your salary" statement. The retort was usually, "Well then, I need a raise."

Whatever police reform means to you, there needs to be an acknowledgement that the system of law enforcement itself is not the main issue. Framing the issue, as I was taught in law school, is the most important first step. After that, you can formulate the analysis and reach the most productive answer.

As a profession, law enforcement has made great strides. Police continue to adapt and evolve in an ever-changing landscape of challenges between criminals as well as social and cultural changes. As more duties get laid at the feet of law enforcement, embracing those pressures and expectations, police work hard to make the communities in which they serve safe and thriving places for all to live, work, and play.

The majority of the men and women of law enforcement I have been fortunate enough to know and work alongside during my career were dedicated, compassionate, and selfless

CHAPTER 10

people. It is often said those who choose to wear the uniform do so because they are dedicated to public service and a higher calling, and it is absolutely true. Sometimes it's important to, at the very least, try to imagine walking in another's shoes. You might just have a moment of clarity.

At the same time, those in law enforcement must also acknowledge that, far too often, the image of the noble profession has suffered from the actions of bad actors or split-second decisions which ended tragically for all involved. Police need to be encouraged and given a clear process to raise concerns about their fellow officers. If law enforcement doesn't police itself, then it faces more scrutiny by the citizenry.

As everyone has witnessed, tragic police citizen encounters sparked concern in communities and ignited loud and insistent calls to reform police tactics and reimagine the delivery of police services. This is a goal police leaders share. I can unequivocally state the policing profession is committed to evolving and building trust within all segments of the community. Society must be willing to listen and discuss the realities of policing, identify meaningful solutions, and understand the trust and support of our communities is the bedrock of successful policing (Renaud, n.d.).

Policing has been around for hundreds of years (See Chapter 2 for origins). The concept of law enforcement is a method of attempting to keep people safe from criminal activity, which has increased, decreased, and evolved over time. The training police officers have been given has changed and developed over time. The equipment law enforcement has at its disposal has become more extensive over time. What now needs further modification, adjustment, and growth are the attitudes of law enforcement officers in relation to how they approach and interact with citizens. In my humble estimation, the Deconfliction method should be a part of the law enforcement evolution. The underlying foundation of the Deconfliction Principles is, in the words of James Dalton in *Roadhouse*, "be nice until it's time not to be nice."

Reiterating, law enforcement as a profession has grown over the years and continues to adapt to changing times. The "thin blue line" of the old days has given way to the "thin blue line of liability." The threat of personal liability for their actions has driven many officers away from law enforcement and keeps many potential recruits from joining. The way forward, which could be difficult, is to implement a national standard for policing related to the training police officers receive. However, any amount of training will not necessarily weed out the potential "bad apples" within law enforcement. Some apples seem pure on the outside, but over time, the inner rot can emerge.

A national police force like in many other countries is probably not an option in the United States. Law enforcement has always been a local endeavor, and a national police force would likely receive immense opposition. Even if a national police force was formed and national standards of policing were established with the most progressive training, tragic police encounters could still occur where officers fail to perform their duties in the utmost humane and professional manner. Does it come down to a very simple answer? Police are human and with it comes the basic human frailties of lack of strength, will, or moral fortitude.

However, the number of horrific incidents resulting from police citizen encounters going horribly wrong could be reduced. Law enforcement needs to focus future training on the mindset of officers. The physical tactics, shooting proficiencies, and practical scenario-based training do not prepare law enforcement officers for the mental and psychological aspect of law enforcement. The need for the Deconfliction Principles with respect to interaction with citizens is great. Law enforcement agencies must begin conditioning officers to mentally prepare for citizen encounters in a way which will keep the situation at a manageable level without the threat of escalating to a point where another type of force is necessary. The public must realize, however, some citizens will not perform their own duty to maintain decorum throughout the encounter with a law enforcement officer.

CHAPTER 10

Deconfliction and the Deconfliction Principles are not about reducing crime, increasing the budgets of police, or defunding the police. Deconfliction is about revealing the truth about law enforcement officers through training and offering a new thought process, a mindset, for officers and citizens to consider when they interact.

It is my belief and hope for Deconfliction to become the very type of training and education which will help change the narrative of police citizen encounters, and police as well as citizens will heed the warning. Don't be a statistic.

REFERENCES

Abramson, A. (2021, July 1). Building Mental Health into Emergency Responses. Apa.org; American Psychological Association. https://www.apa.org/monitor/2021/07/emergency-responses

Allen, J. R. (2020, June 11). Systemic Racism and America Today. Brookings. https://www.brookings.edu/blog/how-we-rise/2020/06/11/systemic-racism-and-america-today/

APA Official Actions Position Statement on Concerns about Use of the Term "Excited Delirium" and Appropriate Medical Management in Out-of-Hospital Contexts. (2020). https://www.psychiatry.org/getattachment/7769e617-ee6a-4a89-829f-4fc71d831ce0/Position-Use-of-Term-Excited-Delirium.pdf

Atherley, L. T., & Hickman, M. J. (2016). Controlling Use of Force: Identifying Police Use of Excessive Force through Analysis of Administrative Records. Policing, 8(2), 123–134. https://www.academia.edu/12677192/Controlling_Use_of_Force_Identifying_Police_Use_of_Excessive_Force_through_Analysis_of_Administrative_Records?email_work_card=

Balfour, M. E., Hahn Stephenson, A., Delany-Brumsey, A., Winsky, J., & Goldman, M. L. (2021). Cops, Clinicians, or Both? Collaborative Approaches to Responding to Behavioral

Health Emergencies. Psychiatric Services, 73(6). https://doi.org/10.1176/appi.ps.202000721

Bell PD. (2022, June 22). Use of Force. Public.powerdms.com. https://public.powerdms.com/BELLPD/documents/1756

Blaivas, M., Shiver, S., Lyon, M., & Adhikari, S. (2006). Control of Hemorrhage in Critical Femoral or Inguinal Penetrating Wounds—An Ultrasound Evaluation. Prehospital and Disaster Medicine, 21(6), 379–382. https://doi.org/10.1017/s1049023x00004076

Bonilla-Silva, E. (1997). Rethinking racism: Toward a structural interpretation. American Sociological Review, 62(3), 465–480. https://doi.org/10.2307/2657316

Braveman, P. A., Arkin, E., Proctor, D., Kauh, T., & Holm, N. (2022). Systemic and Structural Racism: Definitions, Examples, Health Damages, and Approaches to Dismantling. Health Affairs, 41(2), 171–178. https://doi.org/10.1377/hlthaff.2021.01394

Brimbal, L., & Hill, S. (2022, September 19). Rapport Building in Interviews and Interrogations: Translating Research to Practice. National Policing Institute. https://www.policinginstitute.org/onpolicing/rapport-building-in-interviews-and-interrogations-translating-research-to-practice/

Bump, P. (2020, June 7). Over the Past 60 Years, More Spending on Police Hasn't Necessarily Meant Less Crime. Washington Post. https://www.washingtonpost.com/politics/2020/06/07/over-past-60-years-more-spending-police-hasnt-necessarily-meant-less-crime/

Cambridge Dictionary. (2023). SYSTEMIC RACISM | definition in the Cambridge English Dictionary. Dictionary.cambridge.org. https://dictionary.cambridge.org/us/dictionary/english/systemic-racism

REFERENCES

Cidambi, I. (2018, March 30). Police and Addiction. Psychology Today. https://www.psychologytoday.com/us/blog/sure-recovery/201803/police-and-addiction

Cochran, L. L. (2021, July). Police Group Says Ambush Attacks on Officers up 91 Percent over Past Year. The Hill. https://thehill.com/blogs/blog-briefing-%20room/news/561196-police-group-says-ambush-attacks-on-officers-up-91-percent-over/

Colvin, J. (2009, September 3). Brain's "Rage System" Cuts Rational Response. The Globe and Mail. https://www.theglobeandmail.com/news/national/brains-rage-system-cuts-rational-response/article4285675/

Crisp, L. (2021, April 22). "There Wasn't a Whole Lot of Choice": Law Enforcement Expert Reviews Video of Fatal Police Shooting of Ma'Khia Bryant. 10tv.com; WBNS. https://www.10tv.com/article/news/local/there-wasnt-a-whole-lot-of-choice-law-enforcement-expert-reviews-video-of-fatal-police-shooting-of-makhia-bryant/530-7609833b-b2e3-499d-bd63-39bab57da688

Cuncic, A. (2022, December 26). Understanding Inappropriate Affect. Very Well Mind. https://www.verywellmind.com/understanding-inappropriate-affect-4767992

Daigle Law Group. (2020, June 23). Use of Force Continuum – Seriously?? What Is Old Is Now New and What Is New Is Clearly Broken.... DLG Learning Center. https://dlglearning-center.com/use-of-force-continuum-seriously/

De Angelis, J., Rosenthal, R., & Buchner, B. (2016). ASSESSING THE EVIDENCE. https://d3n8a8pro7vhmx.cloudfront.net/nacole/pages/161/attachments/original/1481727974/NACOLE_AccessingtheEvidence_Final.pdf?1481727974

Definition of Key Concepts and Constructs. (2022). In Unjiu.org. United Nations. https://www.unjiu.org/sites/www.unjiu.org/files/jiu_note_2022_1_csws_-_b._questionnaire_annex_-_definitions.docx

Deliso, M. (2021, April 16). What We Know About the Fatal Police Shooting of Daunte Wright. ABC News. https://abcnews.go.com/US/fatal-police-shooting-daunte-wright/story?id=77092274

The Editors of Encyclopedia Britannica. (2016). Thirteenth Amendment | United States Constitution. In Encyclopedia Britannica. https://www.britannica.com/topic/Thirteenth-Amendment

El-Hai, J. (2016, January 4). Screening Police Officers Before They Shoot. Www.linkedin.com. https://www.linkedin.com/pulse/screening-police-officers-before-shoot-jack-el-hai

Elfrink, T. (2020, June 16). "You Can Call Me a Snitch": Police Dispatcher Alerted Supervisor to Officer Kneeling on George Floyd. Washington Post; The Washington Post. https://www.washingtonpost.com/nation/2020/06/16/george-floyd-minneapolis-dispatcher-911/

Encyclopedia Britannica. (2019). Civil Rights Act | Summary, Facts, & History. In Encyclopedia Britannica. https://www.britannica.com/event/Civil-Rights-Act-United-States-1964

Equity vs. Equality and Other Racial Justice Definitions. (2021, April 14). The Annie E. Casey Foundation. https://www.aecf.org/blog/racial-justice-definitions

Foundation, O. (n.d.). Reimagine Policing Pledge. Obama Foundation. https://www.obama.org/my-brothers-keeper-alliance/reimagine-policing/policing-pledge/

Fritscher, L. (2021, October 21). How Parroting Is Used in Therapy. Verywell Mind. https://www.verywellmind.com/parroting-therapeutic-use-2671631

Geller, J. (2019). The Rise and Demise of America's Psychiatric Hospitals: a Tale of Dollars Trumping Sense. Psychiatric News, 54(6). https://doi.org/10.1176/appi.pn.2019.3b29

REFERENCES

Gilson, R. (1995). Special Issue Preface. Human Factors. The Journal of the Human Factors and Ergonomics Society, 37(1), 3–4.

Gladwell, M. (2000). The Tipping Point (p. 6). Little, Brown and Company.

Gladwell, M. (2008). Outliers. Little, Brown and Company.

Green, E., Kuczynski, B., McGuirk, M., & Reichert, J. (2022, October 27). The Effectiveness and Implications of Police Reform: A Review of the Literature. Illinois criminal justice information authority. https://icjia.illinois.gov/researchhub/articles/the-effectiveness-and-implications-of-police-reform-a-review-of-the-literature

Greenville, SC Police Department. (2020). GENERAL ORDER Subject Use of Force by Police Officers. https://www.greenvillesc.gov/DocumentCenter/View/15793/General-Orders---Use-of-Force

The Institute for Criminal Justice Training Reform. (n.d.). State Law Enforcement Training Requirements. The Institute for Criminal Justice Training Reform. https://www.trainingreform.org/state-police-training-requirements

Jefferson, A. (2022, December 15). Atatiana Jefferson: Ex-US Officer Sentenced for Killing Woman in Bedroom. BBC News. https://www.bbc.com/news/world-us-canada-63995243

Johnson, B. (2019, October 31). Psychotherapy: Understanding Group Therapy. American Psychological Association. https://www.apa.org/topics/psychotherapy/group-therapy

Lassiter, M. (2020). I. Civil Rights and Police Brutality, 1957-1963 · Omeka Beta Service. Umich.edu. https://policing.umhistorylabs.lsa.umich.edu/s/detroitunderfire/page/1958-63

Lebow, H. (2021, September 28). Become a Better Listener: Active Listening. Psych Central. https://psychcentral.com/lib/become-a-better-listener-active-listening

Levin, S. (2021, March 11). These US Cities Defunded Police: "We're Transferring Money to the Community." The Guardian. https://www.theguardian.com/us-news/2021/mar/07/us-cities-defund-police-transferring-money-community

Levine, T. R. (2020). Duped: Truth-default Theory and the Social Science of Lying and Deception. University Of Alabama Press.

MacDonald, H. (2020, June 2). The Myth of Systemic Police Racism. Wall Street Journal. https://www.wsj.com/articles/the-myth-of-systemic-police-racism-11591119883

MacDonald, H. (2023, February 19). What Killed Tyre Nichols. City Journal. https://www.city-journal.org/article/what-killed-tyre-nichols

Marker, J. (2012). Teaching 4th Amendment-Based Use-of-Force. https://www.aele.org/law/2012all07/2012-07MLJ501.pdf

Mash, D. C. (2016). Excited Delirium and Sudden Death: A Syndromal Disorder at the Extreme End of the Neuropsychiatric Continuum. Frontiers in Physiology, 7(435), 1. https://doi.org/10.3389/fphys.2016.00435

McIntire, K., & Bowens, J. (2023). Fact Check Team: Cities That Called to "Defund Police" Grappling with Crime Surge Boost. WBMA. https://doi.org/10x2814/2110/960/1446x252/80/7bf3ce99-80c9-4d79-a6c9-10c3a4d82d1b-AP20324825444744

McKay, H. (2014, August 20). Missouri Cop Was Badly Beaten Before Shooting Michael Brown, Says Source. Fox News; Fox News. https://www.foxnews.com/us/missouri-cop-was-badly-beaten-before-shooting-michael-brown-says-source

McKee, A. J. (2024). Broken Windows Theory. In Encyclopedia Britannica. Britannica. https://www.britannica.com/topic/broken-windows-theory

Merriam Webster. (n.d.). Empathy. Merriam-Webster.com. https://www.merriam-webster.com/dictionary/empathy

REFERENCES

Miller, L. (2008). Hostage Negotiation: Psychological Principles and Practices. International Journal of Emergency Mental Health, 7(74), 277–298. https://www.psychceu.com/miller/miller_hostage_neg.pdf

Moore, C. (2015, July 23). Peel's 9 Principles... Are they still relevant? Officer.com; Officer. https://www.officer.com/command-hq/article/12079994/let-magazine-july-2015-on-your-

Mulder, B. (2021, June 14). Fact-check: Have Police Cuts in Austin Led to a "Doubling of Murder"? Austin American-Statesman. https://www.statesman.com/story/news/politics/politifact/2021/06/14/austin-homicides-rise-little-proof-its-tied-police-defunding/7654403002/

National Alliance on Mental Illness. (2023, April). Mental Health by the Numbers. NAMI. https://www.nami.org/about-mental-illness/mental-health-by-the-numbers/

National Archives. (2022, February 8). Civil Rights Act (1964). National Archives. https://www.archives.gov/milestone-documents/civil-rights-act

News, P. (2022, December 15). Texas Officer Convicted for Fatal Shooting of Atatiana Jefferson. PBS News. https://www.pbs.org/newshour/nation/texas-officer-convicted-for-fatal-shooting-of-atatiana-jefferson

Perry, E. (2021, November 8). How to Cultivate a Positive Mental Attitude for Success. Www.betterup.com. https://www.betterup.com/blog/positive-mental-attitude

Plohetski, T. (2021, August 31). How Calls to "Defund the Police" Took Austin to a Crossroads of Police Reform. Www.statesman.com. https://www.statesman.com/in-depth/news/politics/2021/09/01/austin-police-department-budget-cuts-stirs-debate-over-police-reform/5536198001/

Policing Reimagined as Customer Service. (2022). Usdoj.gov. https://cops.usdoj.gov/html/dispatch/12-2022/policing_reimagined.html

Psychiatric Medical Care Communications Team. (2022, October 11). The Difference Between Empathy and Sympathy. Psychiatric Medical Care. https://www.psychmc.com/blogs/empathy-vs-sympathy

Renaud, C. (n.d.). President's Message: Reimagining Policing. Policechiefmagazine.org. Retrieved February 9, 2025, from https://www.policechiefmagazine.org/pres-message-re-imagining-policing/?ref=755131791030300c35a3926057db-ccad

Reynolds, J. (2019, October 4). Police Officer Training: 8 Strategies for De-escalating a Situation. Www.virtualacademy.com. https://www.virtualacademy.com/blog/police-officer-training-8-strategies-for-de-escalating-a-situation

Romero, D. (2019, October 13). Texas Police Officer Shoots Woman to Death Inside Her Home. NBC News; NBC News. https://www.nbcnews.com/news/us-news/texas-police-officer-shoots-woman-death-inside-her-home-n1065451

Ross, D. (2002). Assessment of Graham v. Connor, Ten Years Later | Office of Justice Programs. Www.ojp.gov, 25(2), 294–318. https://www.ojp.gov/. https://doi.org/196233

Sainz, A. (2023, January 28). Memphis Police Disband Unit That Fatally Beat Tyre Nichols. AP NEWS; Associated Press. https://apnews.com/article/politics-memphis-crime-law-enforcement-1b7e8fa4ed7120a897086250d5d6da35

Saladrigas, W. (2020, November 23). Interviews & interrogations: The Delicate Process of Extracting Information. Police1. https://www.police1.com/investigations/articles/interviews-interrogations-the-delicate-process-of-extracting-information-xu89Cz6mKUcKg4xJ/

REFERENCES

Schumaker, E. (2020, July 5). Police Reformers Push for De-escalation Training, But the Jury Is Out on Its Effectiveness. ABC News. https://abcnews.go.com/Health/police-reformers-push-de-escalation-training-jury-effectiveness/story?id=71262003

Sengstock, B., Janet, & Curtis, J. (2022, March 2). Excited Delirium Syndrome - Journal of Paramedic Practice. Journal of Paramedic Practice. https://www.paramedicpractice.com/content/features/excited-delirium-syndrome

Shoichet, C. E. (2014, August 12). Missouri Teen Shot by Police Was Two Days Away from Starting College. CNN. https://www.cnn.com/2014/08/11/justice/michael-brown-missouri-teen-shot/index.html

Stew Smith. (2012, December 5). Delta Force: Missions and History. Military.com. https://www.military.com/special-operations/delta-force.html

Stockton, G. (2021, June 24). 21 States Still Don't Require De-escalation Training for Police. Www.apmreports.org. https://www.apmreports.org/story/2021/06/24/21-states-still-dont-require-deescalation-training-for-police

Tzu, S. (475 C.E.). The Art of War. (Original work published 221 C.E.)

U.S Department of Justice. (n.d.). Community Relations Services Toolkit for Policing Ÿ Understanding Bias: A Resource Guide Bias Policing Overview and Resource Guide. https://www.justice.gov/d9/fieldable-panel-panes/basic-panes/attachments/2021/09/29/understanding_bias_content.pdf

Udaipurwala, S. (2021, June 29). Muscle Memory: Do Your Muscles Really Remember A Skill?» Science ABC. Science ABC. https://www.scienceabc.com/humans/what-is-muscle-memory-new.html

Urofsky, M. (2025). Jim Crow Laws. In Encyclopedia Britannica. https://www.britannica.com/event/Jim-Crow-law

US Supreme Court. (1989). Graham v. Connor, 490 U.S. 386 (1989). Justia Law. https://supreme.justia.com/cases/federal/us/490/386/

Vera, A., & Meilhan, P. (2020, June 16). A 911 Dispatcher Watched Live Surveillance Video of Officers Kneeling on George Floyd and Warned a Supervisor. CNN. https://www.cnn.com/2020/06/15/us/george-floyd-dispatch-audio/index.html

Vigdor, N., & Pietsch, B. (2021, April 21). Teenage Girl Is Fatally Shot by Police in Columbus, Officials Say. The New York Times. https://www.nytimes.com/2021/04/20/us/columbus-ohio-shooting.html

Walsh, C. (2021, February 23). Solving racial disparities in policing. Harvard Gazette; The Harvard Gazette. https://news.harvard.edu/gazette/story/2021/02/solving-racial-disparities-in-policing/

Walters, G. (2020, June 12). These Cities Replaced Cops with Social Workers, Medics, and People Without Guns. Www.vice.com. https://www.vice.com/en/article/y3zpqm/these-cities-replaced-cops-with-social-workers-medics-and-people-without-guns

Wexler, C. (2015, January 30). Testimony by Chuck Wexler. U.S. Department of Justice. http://www.cops.usdoj.gov/pdf/taskforce/submissions/Wexler-Chuck-Testimony.pdf

Wilbanks, W. (1987). THE MYTH OF A RACIST CRIMINAL JUSTICE SYSTEM William Wilbanks Brooks/Cole (a div. of Wadsworth Pub. Journal of Contemporary Criminal Justice, 3(2), 88–93. https://doi.org/10.1177/104398628700300209

REFERENCES

Wilson, J., & Kelling, G. (1982). The Police and Neighborhood Safety Broken Windows. https://media4.manhattan-institute.org/pdf/_atlantic_monthly-broken_windows.pdf

Wooll, M. (2021, August 25). Finding Common Ground with Anyone. BetterUp. https://www.betterup.com/blog/finding-common-ground-with-anyone-a-quick-and-easy-guide

Wright, S. (2022, May 12). How to Talk to Someone Who Is Always Defensive. Psych Central. https://psychcentral.com/lib/how-to-talk-to-someone-who-always-gets-defensive

What's next? Training seminars of the Deconfliction Principles for law enforcement, citizen groups, and corporations.

AUTHOR BIO

Marc Zelinsky started his life's work in 1987 studying criminology at Indiana University of Pennsylvania. He served as an Army Lieutenant, then attended law school at Duquesne University School of Law, graduating in 2001. From there, Marc began a 17-year career in law enforcement in Charleston, South Carolina. Marc went international in 2009-2012 as a police advisor in Afghanistan for 18 months and then spent one year in Haiti. He began his master's in criminal justice while in Afghanistan, finishing in 2012. Marc returned to Charleston as a deputy sheriff where he trained new deputies before becoming a sex crimes detective. Then in 2019, Marc switched from the law enforcement side to the defense as a defense investigator. First, he was part of a team representing a non-911 high value detainee at Guantanamo Bay and later as an Air Force defense investigator. Currently, he is with the Army as a defense investigator. Along the way, Marc attended and graduated from the Federal Criminal Investigator Training Program at the Federal Law Enforcement Training Centers in Glynco, Georgia. You can find Marc offering insight into various topics on Substack, TikTok, Instagram and X. @MrDeconfliction.

Discover more at
4HorsemenPublications.com

10% off using HORSEMEN10

www.ingramcontent.com/pod-product-compliance
Lightning Source LLC
LaVergne TN
LVHW092048060526
838201LV00047B/1287